THE REFERENCE SHELF   VOLUME 40 NUMBER 6

CONFLICT IN THE MIDDLE EAST

EDITED BY
JAMES CHACE

Managing Editor, Interplay

THE H. W. WILSON COMPANY
NEW YORK   1969

THE REFERENCE SHELF

The books in this series contain reprints of articles, excerpts from books, and addresses on current issues and social trends in the United States and other countries. There are six separately bound numbers in each volume, all of which are generally published in the same calendar year. One number is a collection of recent speeches; each of the others is devoted to a single subject and gives background information and discussion from various points of view, concluding with a comprehensive bibliography.

Subscribers to the current volume receive the books as issued. The subscription rate is $14 in the United States and Canada ($17 foreign) for a volume of six numbers. Single numbers are $3.50 each in the United States and Canada ($4 foreign).

PREFACE

The Middle East is the area of the world most likely to become the focal point of struggle among the major powers. The resources of the region, its strategic waterways, the allegiance of its people—these are being sought after and will continue to be fought over by the Western Europeans, the Russians, and the Americans. The ill-fated Suez venture in 1956 when Britain and France, in conjunction with Israel, invaded Egypt because Egyptian president Nasser had nationalized the Suez Canal did not mark the end of European influence as many might have thought. It did, however, open up the area to new possibilities for the Soviet Union and the United States, both of which in certain cases intended to make their influence felt, even perhaps to the point of intervention. Eleven years later, in June 1967, war between Israel and the Middle Eastern powers of Egypt, Syria, Jordan, and Iraq, supported by other members of the Arab League, gave Russia and America new opportunities to make their weight felt. Both countries have endeavored to do so.

Russia has supported the Arab states against Israel without equivocation; the United States has maintained a somewhat neutralist position. The result of this conflict is to create a situation in which tension becomes the order of the day. With Russia attempting to realize its historic dream of ports on the Mediterranean and Indian Ocean and with the Western allies fearful of sea routes to the East being cut off and oil supplies menaced, both East and West find in the Middle East an area in which there is scant hope for meaningful cooperation. There is no unspoken agreement between the United States and the Soviet Union to keep hands off the Middle East; nor is there any agreement that the Middle

East should become a sphere of influence of any particular power.

In a sense, the nations of the Middle East could be termed the "Balkans" of the second half of the twentieth century. In particular, the conflict between Israel and Egypt could involve the great powers to a degree which neither of them would choose. If this seems a bleak estimate of the situation, it is hard to be other than pessimistic. The Arabs are—and are likely to remain—unwilling to accept the result of Israel's victory. The Israelis, fearful of Arab vengeance, will continue to arm, perhaps with nuclear weapons, and it is conceivable that they might even indulge in future pre-emptive strikes.

In the discussions of the Arab-Israeli war that make up the bulk of this book, the editor does not wish to assign blame or decide upon the rightness of the Israeli or Arab cause. As in most wars, right and wrong cannot be easily apportioned. But it is the folly of nations unable to live together in the nuclear age that threatens not only their own peoples but the very existence of civilization.

To any study of the Middle East, two previous Reference Shelf books—*Crisis in the Middle East* (Volume 24, No. 4), edited by Edward Latham, and *The Middle East and the Cold War* (Volume 28, No. 6), edited by Grant F. McClellan —are useful. They tell the story of the Middle East in the postwar era through the last great conflict in 1956. Both books and their bibliographies should be consulted. Moreover, much of the historical background of this troubled corner of the globe can be found in these volumes.

What this book attempts to do is to examine the current struggle in the Middle East as well as to hazard certain judgments as to what the future may portend. The articles have not been chosen in order to reflect the specific views of either the editor or the publisher; rather, they have been chosen in order to illustrate the controversy that surrounds any discussion of this area. The editor gratefully makes acknowledgment to the publishers and authors who have granted permission to reprint material. He would also like to express a special word of thanks to Evelyn Morel for her valuable assistance and encouragement in preparing this work.

JAMES CHACE

November 1968

CONTENTS

ARAB TERRITORY OCCUPIED BY ISRAEL JUNE 1967

I. THE CLIMATE OF CRISIS

EDITOR'S INTRODUCTION

Despite the exploitation of oil resources by the West, despite the former British and French colonial presence in the Levant and operation of the Suez Canal by a privately-owned British-French consortium, the problems which now bedevil the Arab lands cannot be simplistically ascribed to Western economic and political imperialism. Even in those nations, such as Egypt, which have experienced a revolution that expelled the feudal hierarchy, much remains to be done in the way of basic economic and social reform. In fact, the emphasis on military hardware exhibited by so many Arab countries has often prevented economic progress, as leaders attempt not only to find favor with the ruling military cliques but also to distract the masses from their problems at home by exaggerating the danger from abroad.

As F. M. Esfandiary, an Iranian specializing in Middle Eastern social problems, writes in the first article: "The poor live in dilapidated mud huts; the rich landlords in the villages also live in dilapidated mud huts." Money is neither to be enjoyed nor to be used to further economic advancement, but is something to be hidden. So long as the potential wealth of the Middle East lies unused, the welfare of the people will not improve.

But the seeds of social revolution have nevertheless been sown. The main question is whether the revolution is to come from above, as it were, "from the throne" or from below through the guerrilla movements now directed against Israel or from disaffected junior army officers who resent the autocracy of hereditary sheikhdoms. There is indeed a class of "new men" emerging, as the next article, by William Polk, shows; but if these new men form what the Yugoslav Communist writer Djilas has called "the new class," then the replacement of one oligarchy by another is not likely to result in radical social reform.

The threat of Israel—both real and imagined—is that Israel represents a Western state implanted as a hostile body upon the Islamic subcontinent, for modern Israel came into being largely through the immigration of European Jews who quickly displaced the Palestinian Jews as the most dynamic force in postwar Palestine. The success of Israel in becoming an advanced industrial society only highlights the failure of the Arab states in their own quest for modernization.

What remains the most explosive element in Middle Eastern politics may in time also prove the most creative—i.e. Arab nationalism. For, although this nationalist awakening has led to two destructive wars against Israel and to the often short-sighted nationalization of Western economic interests, it is also true that nationalist pride could prove the motive force that could change the social and economic structures of the Middle East into something approaching a modern industrial society. Perhaps it is only in this way that a *modus vivendi* can be reached with an Israel that would no longer seem a threat but rather an aid to stability in a tormented land. At this time, however, in the wake of the Israeli victory of 1967, such a development might well seem a mirage.

MIDDLE EAST PARADOX—THE "BEGGAR RICH" [1]

In recent years, several countries of the Middle East have embarked upon extensive land-reform and other needed programs, which are launched vigorously and enthusiastically, but which soon run into obstacles and resistance and then slowly peter out. The reason is that in their eagerness to obtain quick results and win political acclaim, leaders often forget that the economic problems of the region are inextri-

[1] From article by F. M. Esfandiary, Iranian writer on Middle Eastern social problems. New York *Times Magazine.* p 22+. N. 13, '63. © 1963 by The New York Times Company. Reprinted by permission.

cably tied to deeply rooted traditions and ancient social systems. Basic economic reforms, if they are to succeed, must go hand-in-hand with far-reaching social reorganization. For one of the underlying problems is that, while some are rich and many are poor, the rich are as backward as the poor. . . .

The poor live in dilapidated mud huts; the rich landlords in the villages also live in dilapidated mud huts. The only significant difference is that under the torn and tattered mattresses of the rich rot vast sums of money. They hide money under mattresses, stuff it in colorful quilts or tin cans, salt it away in bank vaults. Some of the more enterprising landlords buy up ever more land, stuff the deeds in their quilts and then have nothing more to do with the acquired property. Money is not something to be enjoyed, it is not for buying comfort and pleasure, it is not for anyone's welfare, it is something to be hidden.

The richest man in Kashan, who is also one of the richest men in Iran, lives in a three-room mud hut, uses old kerosene lamps for light, buys water from a water seller at his door, and in the cold of the night has to cross a neglected plot of land, overgrown with weeds and thistles, to get to the outhouse. His rugs are neatly folded away in the storeroom; when on rare occasions a guest arrives, a couple of the rugs are spread out on the floor of the small reception room, and when the guest leaves the rugs are quickly folded and tucked away again. . . .

The hospitality of the Middle Easterner has always been construed as a sure sign of his generosity. The fact is that the proverbial hospitality of the Middle Easterner arises not so much from generosity as from fear of losing face. Serving abundant food to a guest is a traditional ritual which the Middle Easterner automatically performs even when an unwelcome or despised guest calls. Inhospitality is a stigma which the shame-conscious Middle Easterner tries at all costs to avoid.

Insecurity and Dependence

Along with the insecurity of the Middle Easterner goes his extreme dependence on others. From the moment he is born, he is tightly swaddled and he spends all the rest of his life similarly swaddled by a highly traditional and authoritarian culture, in which it is well-nigh impossible to deviate or to assert independence and autonomy. The landlord's child is breast-fed until he is about two or three years old, cleaned and washed and clothed and sometimes spoon-fed by serfs, servants, and nannies until he is ten or eleven years old. In adolescence, the father, elders, teachers and others are duty-bound to attend to his every need. All he is required to do is to obey.

As a result, the individual, particularly in the provinces, lacks the initiative, the confidence and the sense of responsibility to do anything on his own. The landlord's son leans heavily on his older brothers; the older brothers run to their father each time there is a friction—even a small misunderstanding—with peasants or villagers; the father, however wealthy and influential, meekly submits to the will of the clan head or family patriarch; and the patriarch, himself usually a local chieftain or governor, "will not even drink water" without permission from the central government.

For landlord and peasant alike, the central government is the all-powerful father who is expected to do everything— make all the decisions, shoulder all responsibilities, pay for all reforms. For example, all over the Middle East, wealthy landlords send their children to local village schools. These schools are invariably filthy, deficient and backward; often students have to sit on the damp floors, thirty or forty of them crammed together like sardines, in a small dirty, smelly room that has no window and no light; the teachers are incompetent and ignorant, and the "knowledge" they hammer into the pupils' heads, as a rule outdated.

Most landlords complain about the decrepit schools their children attend, and the deficient education they receive. But if you ask one of these landlords why, with all his wealth and land and influence he does not build a new school for his village and help bring more capable teachers from the city, he will shrug his shoulders and invariably reply that it is not his responsibility to help build a new school for the village, or make any contributions for improvements; it is the government's responsibility to attend to all that.

In Ghazvin, Iran, a disgruntled teacher took me through his school, showing me the dark, foul cells in which children, closely huddled together, studied; he showed me the smelly latrines, the old, broken benches and desks, the schoolmaster's cramped office (in which he also slept at night), the uncovered buckets from which children drank water. As we stopped in each classroom, he indicated various pupils to me and whispered that they were the children of wealthy landlords of that area.

Some of these children come from families who have land as vast as Switzerland [he told me, as we walked in the small courtyard, pursued and oppressed by the foul smell of the latrines]. These families can easily send their children to Europe or America or to Teheran, where they can study at modern schools and receive useful education. But they send them here, to these dirty, frightful schools where, I myself will admit, they learn absolutely nothing—only perhaps a few superstitions.

You'd think the rich people of this area would build a few modern schools and bring educated teachers from Teheran, for their own children, if not for these unfortunate peasant children. But they don't do a damned thing, not a damned thing. We have been begging them for months to give us a plot of land, where at least the children could play and have sports, but they won't even do that.

A rich Syrian family, living on the outskirts of Damascus, throws all its garbage on the street not far from the house. Through the months, the refuse has gathered into an obnoxious little mountain. The family complains of the ungainly sight, the odor and the danger to everybody's health, but when recently a guest asked why they do not hire a private garbage collector, as others have had to do, the master of the house stared at him in surprise and, with memorable inattention to realities, said, "But it's not my responsibility to clear away the dirt; after all, why do we have a government?"

People who have been brought up to feel that everything must be done for them cannot easily be resourceful and independent and do things for themselves, much less for others. The rich landlords in the Middle East hoard their wealth and expect others—relatives, elders, village fathers, the government—to spend money for them. They go through life moaning that they are poor and needy, and they enjoy nothing more than begging for help and for favor. They owe the world nothing, but the world owes them everything.

Also contributing to the parsimony of the Middle Easterner is his acceptance of an austere, confined and pleasureless existence that entails very little spending. Like people of all cultures steeped in tradition, he is comfortable in his discomfort. He groans and grumbles about his plight, swears by all the disciples that he would immediately move away and better his life if only he had the means, but even when he has the means, more often than not he refuses to wriggle out of his cocoon.

Traditions Die Hard

Some time ago, the oil consortium operating in Iran decided to use a part of the island of Kharg in the Persian Gulf as one of its operating centers and build a harbor there to accommodate large foreign tankers. The consortium compensated the islanders generously for the arid land and worthless mud huts it took over. The islanders, ignorant, backward and miserably poor, suddenly found themselves rich. Several among them received ten or fifteen thousand dollars—prodigious sums for this particularly backward area.

These people could have moved to prosperous places—to nearby Bushire, Shiraz or Abadan—they could at long last have created a comfortable life for themselves and their families. Instead, they remained on the scorchingly hot, barren island, moved a couple of hundred meters from their previous homes, and built cramped, dingy, inadequate mud huts

—indistinguishable from the mud huts they had lived in when they were impoverished.

Not far away, in prosperous Kuwait, oil-rich sheikhs build sumptuous marble palaces, import elegant furniture from Europe and America, order expensive clothes and alligator shoes from Rome and Paris and New York, yet continue to walk about barefoot, shun the furniture to sit and sleep on the floor and, rather than use the marble bathrooms, trudge across the field or garden to the old, smelly outhouse.

In . . . [an] Iranian town where . . . [an] old woman prefers begging for alms to spending her own money lives a wealthy landlord who has always walked or used public means of transportation wherever he has wanted to go. In the cold rainy season he and his family struggle on foot through the muddy village roads, and in the heat of summer wait for the bus to visit a neighboring town or inspect one of their own nearby villages.

Some years ago, under relentless pressure from his family and friends, the landlord went to the city and bought a car, a sleek, brand new Cadillac. The car arrived in the small town with much fanfare, people gathered around it, admiring it and congratulating its owner.

The car was seen in town a couple of days, then just as suddenly as it arrived, it disappeared. It was taken to a shed behind the house, carefully covered in quilts and blankets, and it has been sitting there for years. The wealthy landlord and his family continue to walk through mud and slush and dust, and to wait for the bus in rain and heat.

Traditions die hard in these areas. For example it has often been said that the landlord in the Middle East is very unfair to the peasant, cruelly maintaining the feudal system and refusing to alleviate the peasants' misery. This is true. Landlords in the Middle East have tyrannized and exploited the defenseless peasants with impunity. They have flogged peasants for minor offenses, denied them fair shares of the crops, and kept them ignorant and impoverished.

But what is all too often forgotten is that the wealthy landlord in the Middle East has been unfair not only to the peasant; he has also been unfair to himself and to his own children. If he has done nothing for the welfare of his community, neither has he done anything for his own welfare. He has built no schools, hospitals or recreational facilities for the peasant, but he has provided no such services for his own children and family either. And the landlord who flogs his peasants more often than not flogs his own wife and children as well.

Feudal landlords in the Middle East have been trained in a peculiar sterility from which they have been unable to free themselves, much less to free the unfortunate peasants who are trapped with them.

In recent years, a few landlords have moved to the cities, some have even gone abroad to visit, to invest money, perhaps even to settle. Young landlords who have lived and studied abroad refuse to go back to the villages, prefer instead to live in comfortable villas in the cities and benefit from the blessings of progress.

Others who have spent years abroad go back to the inherited land, defy tradition, treat the peasant fairly and democratically and, rather than hoard their money, invest in constructive projects, make donations for public welfare, build schools and hospitals, start factories and industries. In areas where land reform is being vigorously pushed, this auspicious trend has been given additional impetus.

But the majority of wealthy landlords in the Middle East still hoard their money and do nothing for their own welfare or the welfare of the peasants and villagers who grovel on their properties. So long as this prodigious wealth lies dormant, the countries of the Middle East will remain poor, and social progress will, at best, be slow. A more liberal educational system and, above all, basic changes in our familial institutions, vigorously launched and pushed by the central governments, will, in the long run, induce in coming generations the sense of security, confidence, responsibility and initiative essential to a dynamic economy and to progress. The wealth is here now, among the people; needed is the strength to get up and benefit from this wealth.

TRADITION AND THE NEW ELITE [2]

To attempt to bridge . . . [the] gap between theory and reporting, I would like to set out one relatively simple conceptual scheme for the political analysis of social change. If this scheme has utility, it is primarily in enabling reporters to ignore large elements of society and to concentrate their efforts on relatively few points of high political leverage. Its application is probably confined to developing societies and may not be relevant in many of those. It is extrapolated primarily from my observations in Iran, Turkey, Iraq, Egypt, Algeria, and Morocco.

Essentially, there are two general categories of social analyses. One category relates primarily to horizontal divisions between classes; the other category relates to groups of people within a given society. The first analysis has been used primarily for the more advanced societies; the second for more primitive societies.

By drawing three horizontal lines, with linear projections to indicate population size in each class, one can get a profile of American society, for example, which shows the tremendous preponderance of the middle class. The factors which make up this class differentiation can be grouped psychologically, economically, politically, and in other ways coherently and satisfactorily. A further refinement can be obtained by drawing vertical lines to divide off certain ethnic and religious groups which can then be separately considered.

In viewing such composite societies as that of Lebanon, a class analysis requires so many vertical lines, with consider-

[2] From the article "The Middle East: Analyzing Social Change," by William R. Polk, professor of history and director of the Center for Middle Eastern Studies, University of Chicago; former member of the Policy Planning Council of the State Department; author of *The United States and the Arab World*. *Bulletin of the Atomic Scientists*. 23:12-19. Ja. '67. The article is reprinted with permission from the January 1967 issue of the *Bulletin of the Atomic Scientists*. Copyright 1967 by the Educational Foundation for Nuclear Science.

able differentiation between the groups, as to be too cumbersome to use. Consequently, most political analyses of such a society as the Lebanese concentrate on groups, treated separately. When, however, reasonably rapid social change begins to take place, one finds a considerable intermingling of the social groups and the development of some coherence of class, occupational, and geographical interests. For this reason, a political analysis of even such a small complex society as Lebanon can be extraordinarily difficult.

The overwhelming number of cases in the underdeveloped countries, however, are not as complex as Lebanon. Most of the countries have a clearly defined dominant group. Many have thought of this group as an "elite" or a "new middle class." Both of these concepts leave out much that is economically and politically crucial. Here I will argue that the key political differentiation in this case is between the "traditional" elements of the society and what I have called the "new men."

The "new men" are those who possess the skill, the discipline, the orientation, and the motivation to modernize society. However much they may differ among themselves in terms of income, education, and ability, they are even more sharply differentiated, in politically more significant ways, from the traditional elements of society.

The "New Men" in Egypt

For example, Egypt today is a country of approximately 28 million people. Of these about 25 million are Sunni Muslim and 3 million are Copts. The vast majority of the population, between 60 and 75 per cent, are dependent upon agriculture either directly or indirectly as a means of subsistence. The GNP [Gross National Product] of Egypt is $3.5 billion. The GNP per capita is approximately $120. The rise of GNP per capita has been extremely small in the past. Indeed, it has been largely offset by the rapid (3 per cent) rise of the population. In the last two or three years the rise of the GNP per capita has been between 2 and 3 per cent. In previous years, there was no statistical rise at all. Meanwhile, expectations have risen, and continue to rise, sharply. Yet, the regime remains stable.

Obviously, what this calls for is some categorization—"disaggregation"—of information. The scheme which appears to make the most sense to me is one which essentially divides the society into six compartments. The compartments to the right represent the traditional society; to the left, the modern component.

	NEW MEN		TRADITIONAL SOCIETY	

In Egyptian society, perhaps 85 per cent of the population is traditional lower class. There is, as yet, no real political differentiation between the rural and urban components. Indeed, the urban component of the traditional lower class appears to form itself into urban "villages" within cities, and rural villages develop urban extensions. These people take part in relatively few functions of urban life and remain isolated from urban political movements.

Rural lower class society remains fragmented in village communities or in kinship groups within village communities. Thus, extreme dissatisfaction with an existing political situation, as reported in Egypt between the end of World War II and the coup d'état of 1952, results in sporadic upsurges of violence and dissidence but not in any organized militancy.

The middle box on the traditional side is composed of merchants, people educated in traditional subjects such as Islamic law and Arabic literature, owners of medium-sized plots of land, and others who, while educated, are not qualified in subjects which orient them toward a modern society.

Like the traditional lower class, the middle class traditional society is both urban and rural based. In Egypt, its members number, at a guess, about 10 per cent of the population.

The top box on the traditional side has dwindled considerably in Egypt since land reform was instituted in 1952. Prior to land reform there were approximately 5,000 "proprietors" of land in units of over one hundred acres. However, a number of these "proprietors" were in fact duplications since a single person might be proprietor over several pieces of land.

If one accepts this arbitrary definition of the landed component of the upper class (one hundred acres of irrigated land in 1945 would yield approximately $12,500 of rent), the traditional Egyptian upper class may be estimated at about 1 per cent of the population.

Trying to Create a Modern Society

Egypt has made several attempts to create a modern component of its society. The first, the most dramatic and rapid, was from approximately 1820 to 1840; the second, over which native Egyptians exercised less direction and which was less consciously undertaken or concentrated, took place from approximately 1900 to the beginning of World War II; and the third, now in process, began shortly after the 1952 coup d'état.

In the first period, the great Turkish governor of Egypt, Mehemet Ali Pasha, attempted to create in Egypt a movement of modernization somewhat similar to the Meiji of Japan [reign of Emperor Mutsuhito, 1868-1912]. Power, Mehemet Ali realized, meant more than having uniformed soldiers and modern guns—which could be dangerous and expensive—but meant also having the means to clothe and feed soldiers, to make and supply guns, and to organize and control the soldiers. This meant building factories, training people to run them, acquiring the financial power to pay for them.

In his attempt to modernize Egyptian society, Mehemet Ali dispossessed traditional landowners, destroyed the medieval guild system, crushed the Mamluk aristocracy [soldiers recruited from slaves converted to Islam who had great political power in Egypt 1250-1517], largely replaced the traditional handicraft industry, altered the agricultural crop system, and sent large numbers of students, technicians, and potential industrial workers to Europe for training.

By 1841, Mehemet Ali had a modern, disciplined military force of nearly 200,000 men, a relatively large textile industry, dockyards and arsenals sufficient to supply his growing and powerful navy, and about 30,000 industrial workers.

Mehemet Ali's attempt at modernization failed primarily due to Western intervention. In 1840 Great Britain invaded Lebanon and Syria, which were then part of the Egyptian Empire, and drove out the Egyptians. The Egyptian state was also forced to give up tariff barriers and a domestic commercial monopoly, and to reduce its army.

This experiment is of more than antiquarian interest for two reasons. First, it shows that once the intense drive of modernization stops, the new and the traditional are apt to meld into a new pattern. The sharp division of the new from the traditional fades as the new acquires some of the vested interests of the old, and new elements will gradually develop to the left. Thus the arbitrary, analytical division of new and traditional society can be seen to be historically fluid; indeed, from a cultural point of view, it may be the movement between categories which is of most interest. Second, even an abortive thrust toward modernization can lay the groundwork for subsequent development and probably does destroy the old structure of power so that it cannot be reimposed.

Three basic policies can be noted in Egypt since 1952 which have tended to transplant people from the lower right-hand into the lower left-hand box of our diagram.

The first of these was an attempt to redistribute rural income through land reform. This policy had two effects: It stripped away financial power in large part from the upper class traditional society—the top right-hand box. That group had held political power and was the principal initial rival of Nasser's new regime. It was also a step toward raising the standard of living of the traditional lower class to the point where some elements of the lower class would become amenable to modernization.

The Egyptian government early recognized that this policy had not been entirely successful. Probably no more conservative man than the Egyptian peasant is alive today. Therefore, the regime undertook a second program to create a new sort of Egyptian peasant. This was the essence of the "Liberation Province" scheme in Egypt. While this scheme has not been successful economically, it has been sporadically pursued by the Egyptian government because of the political importance of the social goals.

The "new man" of Liberation Province was marked off from the traditional Egyptian peasant by a standardized uniform in place of the traditional gown, by a much higher caloric intake of food, and by a salary four times the average rate in upper Egypt. In addition, the workers were to put their children into a boarding school, in some ways similar to the practice in the Israel *kibbutzim*, which presumably would enable teachers to insure a more modern upbringing for the children. Moreover, like the rest of Egypt, Liberation Province was to become a mixed rural and industrial economy with factories interspersed throughout the agricultural area.

The third thrust of Egyptian policy has been toward industrialization. Repeatedly and consistently American and other advisers have warned the Egyptian government that it was making a tragic economic mistake in promoting industry rather than agriculture in its development scheme. It was pointed out to the Egyptian government that Egyptian infant industry could never compete on the world market and that the building of such monuments as the Helwan Steel Factory was a frivolous if prestigious waste of critically short Egyptian resources. What Egypt needed, in the opinion of the advisers, was to concentrate on exportable agricultural commodities which would increase foreign exchange earnings.

The Egyptian government has consistently refused to follow Western advice and has devoted an overwhelming proportion of its resources to the industrialization of the society. Undoubtedly, from an economic point of view, Western advice was sound. However, the Egyptian government's actions have responded to political criteria.

Shortly after the 1952 coup, the new Egyptian rulers realized that they must weaken their opponents, the traditional ruling class, and they accomplished this through a series of steps—from land reform, to the banning of the established political parties, to eventual nationalization of most business ventures. It was some time later, however, before the "Free Officers" acted to build a new constituency for their regime. In their attempts to do this, through land reform and the Liberation Province scheme, they were disappointed. It was clear that the transformation of the peasant was going to be a long and frustrating process.

Probably for other reasons, the new rulers set about creating an industry, but once having embarked on this policy they came to realize that industry is of the modern world. The people properly and fully associated with it are, obviously, on the left side of the dividing line. Not until they became a large and secure group could the regime be powerful and secure. A detailed analysis of the Egyptian development plan will show conclusively that the political intent was clearly to move people from the right side of the ledger to the left of the modern component of Egyptian society. This could be done only if large numbers of jobs were created in elements of the economy which were oriented toward modern society. Politics, not economics, set the policy.

The Army's Role

In addition to creating niches in the modern sector, the regime had to create the "new men" to fill them. Essentially, Egypt has used two methods of accomplishing this transition.

The first, education, is slow and costly, but ultimately the most productive. In 1945, approximately 900,000 Egyptians attended school. By 1960, this number had been more than trebled, and by 1970 it will reach nearly six million. Technical education was virtually a product of the 1952 revolution. By 1961, nearly 40,000 Egyptians had graduated from Egyptian universities in the natural sciences and technology. Nearly 120,000 were then in training in vocational schools in Egypt.

The second method was enforced military service. It was, above all, the army which was the vanguard and source of the revolution in Egypt. It was not until nearly the end of the nineteenth century that native Egyptians were able to rise to senior ranks in the Egyptian army. It was not until the eve of World War II that the military academy was opened to young men of the lower middle class: among the first cadets was Gamal Abd'n-Nasir—Nasser.

The armies alone among the institutions of the under-developed societies were organized along nationalist, modern lines without commitments to the past. The military alone had a defined code, a clear line of command, lines of communications, mobility, force, and, ultimately, will. The better it became as a modern instrument of the state, the less committed it was to the traditional state.

In Egypt today the army is not only a "school" in civic virtues, but is in addition a school to impart modern skills, a hospital to cure the ills of society by turning out healthier men, and a source of discipline. Each year, approximately 20,000 Egyptians are inducted into the army for three-year enlistments. From 1957 to 1961, about 130,000 Egyptians passed out of the armed forces into civilian life. When one considers that larger scale, modern Egyptian industry in 1961 employed roughly a quarter of a million workers, the impact of this output of ex-soldiers can be appreciated.

It appears relatively certain that few of the soldiers have returned to the right side of the column, the traditional society. The reason is simple: these ex-soldiers are possessed of rudimentary technical training, a sense of discipline, an indoctrination in nationalism, and certainly a far higher standard of health than those who have not had their army experience. All of these are rare and prized possessions in a backward, poor but rapidly evolving and industrializing society. Even more basic is the transformation of simple instruction in health—when a man knows what bilharzia is he cannot any longer be a Nile peasant. The army can thus be seen to be a primary agent in the creation of the group of "new men" who fit in the lower left-hand box of our scheme.

The creation of the other two boxes on the left hand side of the column is almost a mechanical process consequent to the development of the lower left-hand box. Former noncommissioned officers and those with industrial experience have become the foremen and the technicians who mobilize the industrial labor force. Officers are increasingly relied upon by the Egyptian government for positions in the government, commercial, and industrial bureaucracies.

The Egyptian government's political program of nationalizing industry has served both to weaken the control of rival groups in the society, particularly by the urban component of the traditional upper class, and to create positions for this new bureaucratic middle class.

Finally, the upper left-hand box in our scheme is composed of the senior administrators, technicians, bureaucrats, and officials of the Egyptian regime. In many ways, this group has already acquired the accouterments of political and social power that formerly pertained to the traditional upper class. Such men as the directors of the Suez Canal Authority and the Petroleum Authority, the senior officials in the presidency, governors of provinces, and the director of the steel factory have relatively great affluence and power. At the pinnacle of this column is Nasser himself.

An analysis of Egyptian politics over the last ten years and a projection of plans for the coming decade would indicate that the primary policy of the Egyptian government is to shift the vertical line increasingly to the right so that a larger proportion of the Egyptian population is included in the categories of "new men." With this primarily political purpose in mind, the developmental policies of the Egyptian government appear reasonably consistent, coherent, and well conceived.

The question of whether or not the Egyptian government can afford to sustain this program is a crucial one. Much, of course, depends upon the extent of foreign aid Egypt can command. In general, however, at the current rate of expenditure and the current levels of foreign aid, the momentum can only be sustained if the foreign debt can be rolled over virtually continuously. At some point, major changes either in the allocations or in the revenues will have to be made.

It is important to understand that the economic crises—and the budgetary maneuvers these will entail—may themselves be significant forces of change as well as of inhibition. A government may be driven either to a more radical policy, or may be replaced by those who will claim to be able to do a better job.

When one uses this scheme to analyze political stability, various new factors emerge. In the first place, it is evident that GNP per capita is not a politically useful measure. GNP per capita can remain stable, rise, or be lowered with stability, tension, or revolution. But very different results are obtained from a sectoral analysis.

Prior to the 1952 coup, when the upper two right-hand boxes in our scheme were dominant in Egypt, a precipitous change in their income might have been reflected in serious political disturbance. Today that is no longer the case. Since 1952, the income of the upper and middle traditional classes has fallen as their political power has declined. While most still live well by any standards, they no longer hold a commanding position in the Egyptian economy. Conversely, a precipitous downward change in the income in any one of the three left-hand boxes might today produce considerable political unrest.

In pre-1952 Egypt, the two upper right-hand groups controlled the economy, the press, the security forces, and the bureaucracy. Today, the various kinds of power are exercised by the new men.

Somewhat over 80 per cent of the Egyptian population is in the traditional lower class. While this group does enjoy somewhat better health today than half a century ago, and does have some access to schooling which it did not have until recently, its per capita income has always hovered near subsistence. Today, as it has always been, this group is politically irrelevant.

What of the new men? We do not know in detail, but it is clear that the real income of all three modern classes has risen sharply since 1952. These groups have been the principal beneficiaries of economic growth and reallocation. Indeed, virtually all of the new men are the children of the revolution.

It is fairly clear, therefore, that while the performance of the government as a whole has been deficient economically, it has been quite able to satisfy those who count politically.

THE SHAH'S "REVOLUTION" [3]

Mohammed Riza Pahlevi, Shahinshah (Shah of Shahs) of Iran, has stepped off his Peacock Throne. That bejeweled emblem of pomp and empire is stored away in a downtown bank vault. At the palace, the Shah has turned his attention to the more plebeian matters of what he calls a "white revolution."

After 2,500 years time has run out for feudal Iran and the Shah knows it. Someone is going to lead his country out of archaic stagnation and he wants to be remembered as the leader of that march, not as possibly the last king of the world's oldest monarchy. He is determined to be his own Nasser.

[3] From "Iran's Shah Leads a 'White Revolution,'" by Jay Walz, staff correspondent. New York *Times Magazine.* p23+. O. 27, '63. © 1963 by The New York Times Company. Reprinted by permission.

Whether the Shah will succeed in his purpose of transforming Iran into a self-reliant, self-confident modern nation in the Western mold is still uncertain. Undeniably, he has made some progress, but even well-wishers feel his programs have been hastily conceived, and they have aroused bitter opposition among many powerful elements in Iran.

The fact that any reform program at all has taken so long getting started is a comment on Iran, its people and its political and social state.

Iran is a land of 628,000 square miles—about the size of the United States east of the Mississippi River—with 21 million inhabitants. Although about three quarters of the land is too mountainous and arid for farming, the Shah is probably not overoptimistic in estimating that his country could support "three times our present population at the European standard of living."

Fertile hillsides around the Caspian shore produce excellent fruit, vegetables, rice and tea, although the area is more famous perhaps for the caviar that comes from the sea thereabouts. The semiarid plains of Khurasan and Fars grow wheat, cotton and sugar beets.

Underground water reserves have been largely unexplored but are known to exist extensively. So, too, exist deposits of minerals, notably iron and coal. And Iran is one of the world's major oil producers. The oil fields have been nationalized since 1951, under the administration of the National Iranian Oil Company, which deals with a consortium of foreign oil firms. This year, a record half-billion barrels of crude oil are in prospect and Iran's fifty-fifty share of the profits may well be $400 million.

Little of this wealth, however, trickles past the politicians and bureaucrats to the people. In spite of $750 million in American economic aid over the past decade, the average family income is $170 a year. The population is 80 per cent rural (10 per cent live in Teheran and 10 per cent in smaller cities) and 80 per cent illiterate. The countryside is sparsely and primitively settled. Roads and communications are crude.

A few tribes—the Lur in the west and the Bakhtiari in the central Zagros Mountains, the Kurds in northwestern Azerbaijan and the Turkmen in northeast Khurasan—cluster around isolated water holes or live a seminomadic life, fighting each other for grazing fields and warding off outsiders. But most rural Iranians are farmers—or, more properly, serfs, working not for themselves but for great absentee landlords. A few years ago, it could be said Iran was owned by not more than one thousand families. Their holdings were enormous.

The Feudal Tradition

The Shah's father, Riza Shah Pahlevi, was not a rich man to begin with, but during his reign he became Iran's largest landowner, with more than two thousand villages. Others were not far behind. It was traditional for ministers of state and parliamentary deputies and senators to come from "the thousand families."

Feudalism was so fixed a tradition that only five years ago the Shah found it necessary, in the interest of progress, to invoke a decree ordering landlords to stop taking gifts, such as chickens, eggs and "marriage dues" from peasants. When a landlord's daughter married, it was the custom for all his peasants to pour in gifts of animals and produce—sometimes for good measure, a month or two of labor. When a peasant's daughter married, her father paid the landlord a fee. When he quarreled with his neighbor, he was subject to a fine to his landlord.

Why the peasants did not revolt long ago is still a question. Certainly, they would not have stood such inequality much longer in these days of airplane travel and transistor radios. The Shah decided it would be better to act while he retained the choice of decision.

The "white revolution" is based on a six-point program. Briefly it calls for land redistribution, profit sharing for factory workers, nationalization of forests, a literacy corps, the sale of some state factories to help finance the program and electoral reforms, including woman suffrage. Land redistribution is the key issue by which the program will succeed or fail.

The Shah's intention is that ultimately all farm land in Iran will be broken up into individually owned plots ranging in size from a maximum of 100 to 600 acres, depending upon its fertility. The former landlords are to be paid—in ten annual installments—a price based on former tax assessments, the taxes actually collected and the income derived from the peasants. The farmers themselves are to repay the government over a fifteen-year period.

So far, officially, the lands surrounding 8,000 villages, with a tax value of $86 million have been purchased from former landlords, and those of 6,000 villages have been distributed to 230,000 peasant families, representing a population of 1.2 million. But Iran has some 50,000 villages. Obviously, only the surface has been scratched.

Furthermore, cooperative agencies to take the place of the landlords must be established—to supply seeds, fertilizer, equipment, loans and help in marketing. The development of such cooperatives is not keeping pace with redistribution, but without helping hands the inexperienced peasant owner will not be able to use his land efficiently for several years.

In that event, food production may fall, peasants become disillusioned and millions go hungry. The consequences could be disastrous to the Shah. The outcome will be touch and go for at least five years.

As an indication of the problems, there is the case of a village in Azerbaijan. Reformers from Teheran tried to introduce a modern combine harvester. The villagers, who for hundreds of years had been allowed to pick up the gleanings, were enraged by the machine, which left none. They burned the combine.

One land-reform official was murdered in Fars Province last winter. He may have been a victim of bandits seeking clothes and food, or he may have blundered into the rival grazing claims of local tribes. The Shah considers him a martyr to reform.

For their part, the landlords are far from reconciled. Charges abound that the Shah is a traitor to his class, exploiting the peasants for political expediency—that he is promising the peasants more than he can deliver and will suffer disaster when they become disillusioned. The landlords are supported by some Teheran bankers when they complain that the government will not—indeed cannot—keep its promise to pay the landlords for so much land. This, they say, is just one tragic consequence of having rushed into land reform, pell-mell, without careful planning.

It is perhaps only natural that the landlords should protest they have not been paid fair prices for the land taken from them, but the Shah pooh-poohs their cries of anguish.

What do they expect? [he asks]. The government is paying them what they themselves let the land be assessed at for years, when they paid their taxes. They never complained before that assessments were too low.

Landlords—and bankers—are not the only opponents of the Shah's program. "Black reactionary" is an epithet he uses with increasing frequency these days, and it is directed most vehemently against the Shiite mullahs, the ultraconservative Muslim leaders, who not only oppose land redistribution but say that the emancipation of women defies Islamic law. . . .

The size of the army is a frequent source of criticism. With United States aid, the Shah has built it up to 200,000 men. His American military advisers argue that a smaller force could be more efficient. Many Iranians believe its real function is "to protect the throne."

One veteran observer of the imperial court says he is dismayed by the Shah's "almost complete reliance" on the army and on his secret police, the Savak, for information. Too often, it is feared, the generals isolate the Shah from unpleasant facts and close his ears to constructive criticism. During the past crucial year, for example, the execution of the reform program has been in the hands of the mild Premier Asadollah Alam. He was chosen for the job largely because he is a completely unquestioning supporter of the Shah, a friend since their school days together.

Some critics declare the Shah's only interest in reform is his hope of perpetuating the monarchy for his new son and heir. Certainly the Shah's new approach has been more evident since the birth of Crown Prince Riza . . . [in 1960]. But any king naturally hopes to perpetuate the kingdom.

Skepticism is frequently voiced by educated Iranians in places of responsibility in government and the professions, partly perhaps because one Iranian is always reluctant to trust another. They fear the Shah has plunged blindly into an adventure of political fortune. Not a few doubt he intends to fight to the finish; they predict he will relapse once he has reaped the rewards of showing himself "a hero to the peasants."

"This land-reform stunt was ill-conceived and not planned at all. It will not work," said a Teheran businessman bitterly.

Portrait of a Ruler

The Shah . . . may be said to be near the midpoint of his life and career. He began his reign in 1941, a bright, handsome youth with a European education and a supreme lack of confidence in his own ability to fill the shoes of his domineering father. He retains his youthful and athletic leanness, although his dark, wavy hair is graying, but he has developed an air of complete self-assurance.

His smile is totally disarming. Doing away with stuffy formality, he walks around his desk to greet visitors with a smile and a handshake as they enter his office. To an American, he speaks vernacular English, punctuated with an occasional slang phrase. "So what?" he will say when he takes exception to something.

But a new seriousness has come over him. The lines of his face cut deeper grooves than they used to. His thin lips move tautly, his gaze sharpens and his voice becomes more authoritative as he discusses his plans.

My job is to prepare my country for democracy [he told a recent visitor], but we cannot yet have democracy—American or British style. It is not the time.

I suppose in time we might have a monarchy such as they now have in Britain or Sweden—when a king might play a different role [i.e., reign not rule]. But our people are not ready for that. Our people need the King. Without the King, Iran would have been gone long ago.

Some Western correspondents who come here do not realize that discipline is still required in my country. Without discipline we cannot have a revolution like this.

He speaks passionately of land reform:

It will be completed because the people demand it. We have started it. We cannot turn back. The people will not let anyone, even those who give lip service to reform, stop it.

His journeys around the country have obviously convinced him this is so. Everywhere, peasants have greeted him with wild acclaim, and such popularity is a heady brew. The sour opposition of landlords and mullahs and Teheran skeptics has not spoiled his enjoyment of his new friendship with the mass of his countrymen.

It can be argued that the only way to accomplish land reform is to plunge into it as the Shah has done. It would take years to prepare Iran completely for this desperately necessary change, and then it might well be too late. The Shah has many supporters who believe that action—abrupt, sometimes mistaken, often fumbling, but action—to right the injustices of its ancient system of landholding is Iran's greatest need.

Through it all, the Shah, if he really wants to win his "election" as leader in fact as well as in name, must build new confidence among his people in new ways of life. For "black reactionaries" have not been the only enemies of reform and change. The traditional Persian cynicism and apathy have been a paralytic disease for centuries. To get

Iran moving, the Shah will need to ride a white charger of mythical endurance and speed.

SAUDI ARABIA LEAPS FORWARD [4]

By Saudi Arabia's Islamic calendar, this year is 1386, and visitors to the desert kingdom often feel that is about where Saudi Arabia stands on the Western calendar. Justice still decrees an eye for an eye. Marriages are arranged sight unseen. A few weeks ago the deputy rector of the Islamic University at Medina even came out in support of a fourteenth century theory that the world is flat and mountains are only ballast to keep it from tipping over. But for all this, Saudi Arabia's old ideas and old ways are giving way to the twentieth century. King Feisal ibn Abdul Aziz, sixty-two, is not afraid to call it a revolution. "Revolutions," he says, "can come from a throne as well as from a conspirator's cellar."

Across the country, new hospitals, schools, housing projects and factories are sprouting up on the hot horizon. In the privacy of their homes, many Saudis no longer fear that drinking, dancing or a little poker will bring down the wrath of Allah—or the government. Out in the desert, the country's ever-wandering Bedouins, who comprise 80 per cent of Saudi Arabia's 3.5 million people, are swapping their camels for Land Rovers and pickup trucks, and—thanks to a government well-drilling program that guarantees them water—are abandoning their nomadic ways and settling into community life.

In the process, a true nation is emerging out of what once was four major tribal confederations and two or three urban centers. As its leader, Feisal himself was his own best proof of the change. . . . In his flowing white robes and gold headband, he flew off to Spain for five days of trade and foreign-investment talks with Francisco Franco. From Madrid he goes on to Washington . . . where he will meet with President Johnson to discuss economic development and other

[4] From "Saudi Arabia: Revolution from the Throne." *Time*. 87:45. Je. 24, '66. Copyright Time Inc. 1966. Reprinted by permission.

problems of the Middle East. In the old days of Saudi extravagance, there would have been one plane for the King, another for his luggage and 100 to 150 traveling companions. This time there were only one black, green and white Saudi Arabian Airlines Boeing 720B and a mere nine assistants.

Riches to Work

Unlike his profligate half-brother—ex-King Saud, whom he nudged aside in 1964 after Saud had all but bankrupted the country—Feisal is an energetic, reform-minded ruler determined to put Saudi Arabia's oil riches to work for the people. No sooner was he in power than he ordered free education and medical service for all Saudis, stepped up oil production and trimmed the country's budget. Today Saud's lavish, pink-walled Nasiriyah Palace in Riyadh—with an air-conditioning system said to be second in size only to the Pentagon's—lies deserted.

Feisal lives instead in a smaller economy model. Saud's beloved fleet of Cadillacs has given way to a pair of Chrysler New Yorkers, and with a deftly democratic touch, Feisal always sits up front next to the driver. To get just as close to the people, Feisal holds a daily *majlis* (assembly) and invites everyone—from the richest merchant to the scruffiest Bedouin —to come and get his gripes off his chest. "We believe," says Feisal, "that we represent democracy in its highest form, though its structure may be alien to Western ways."

And to Saudi ways, as well. Feisal puts in a twenty-hour day, personally studies every new government project, and deals harshly with loafers. . . . Even tougher is Feisal's able younger brother Prince Sultan, his forty-one-year-old defense minister, who recently demanded that Feisal fire fully 75 per cent of the ministry workers for tardiness after the long *hajj* (pilgrimage) holiday this spring. As for anyone found taking a bribe, Sultan says he will personally demand the culprit's execution.

The Social Revolution

Even more far-reaching—though more subtle—is the social revolution overtaking Saudi Arabia. Many Saudi women now sport lipstick, eye shadow and slacks under their shapeless black shrouds and dark veils. Their daughters are going to school for the first time. Any student—male or female—who can win admission to a foreign university receives full expenses and a generous living allowance. Of his own eight sons, Feisal has sent the youngest seven abroad for schooling, including his bright, second oldest son Prince Mohamed bin Feisal, twenty-nine, the country's first royal prince ever to graduate from a university anywhere.

In a crash road-building program, Feisal plans six thousand miles of new roads by 1970. He is also rebuilding the Hejaz Railway—in ruins ever since Lawrence of Arabia blew it apart during World War I—from Medina through Jordan to Syria. In Jeddah, he is putting up a $14 million water-desalting plant that will daily convert Red Sea water into 5 million gallons of potable water and produce 45,000 kilowatts of power.

A few years ago under Saud, radios were barely tolerated. Today almost every family has one, and last year Feisal even introduced television—though a heavily edited version in which Dodge City cowpokes swagger up to the bar and demand "a shot of lemon squash." Even the land's harsh justice is being relaxed—in a quiet Saudi way. Rather than being beheaded, murderers are simply shot nowadays. Thieves still may lose a hand; but it is first pumped with painkillers, the wrist is wrenched from the socket to avoid any broken bones, and the hand is amputated with sterilized instruments rather than with one grisly swipe of an ax.

Cairo's Hostility

How far Feisal can go with his revolution will depend to some extent on the course that Gamal Abdel Nasser takes in the Middle East. . . . [Because of Egyptian antagonism] Feisal estimates that he must spend more than $1.5 billion for defense over the next . . . [few] years. Money is no problem. This year [1966] Feisal expects to pump almost 1 billion barrels of oil, worth $750 million to the government, which would put his country ahead of Kuwait as the world's biggest producer. . . .

Almost nightly, Cairo radio rakes Feisal as "the bearded bigot" and the "Pope of Islam." "We hear someone who says he is pursuing the way of unity," Nasser sneered of Feisal. . . . "But we find he is in effect unifying reactionary forces." Feisal replies calmly to such attacks. "My task," he once said, "is with my people and my country, not with others."

THE PERSIAN GULF DILEMMA [5]

Two of the nine rulers of British-protected states in the Persian Gulf area have now been deposed. They are the first victims of a campaign to resist the rapid growth of republican feeling among the 316,000 people living there, by removing some of the worst excesses of Arabian monarchy.

In August . . . [1966], Sheikh Shakbut, at the age of sixty-one and after a fairly peaceful reign of thirty-eight years, was expelled from his small but rich oil kingdom of Abu Dhabi. A man whose grasping lust for money caused comment even among his fellow sheikhs, he has lost, at the same time as his kingdom, his income from oil royalties, totaling $5.5 million a month.

As soon as the deposition order had been signed, the RAF flew him hurriedly from the national airport—a strip of beaten sand, a customs hut, and a wind sock—to Bahrein. There Sheikh Isa, the young and unsure ruler who is rumored to be the next on the British list of rulers to be dismissed, granted him exile with reluctance, perhaps fearing that by associating with his guest, he might further weaken his own position.

[5] Report, "Middle East II: Persian Gulf," by Martin Page, a British freelance writer. *Atlantic.* 219:38+. Ap. '67. Copyright © 1967, by The Atlantic Monthly Company, Boston, Mass. Reprinted with permission.

When Shakbut was safely out of the way, the British authorities announced that he had been deposed by his family for "failing to create a proper administration and not using the kingdom's wealth for the benefit of the people." While formally denying that Britain had played any part in the coup d'état, its Acting Political Resident in the Persian Gulf area, Hugh Balfour-Paul, did not find it inconsistent with his status as a diplomat to add that the old sheikh had displayed "a manifest inability to govern properly."

One bar against accepting these statements at face value is that they ignore the visit to the foreign office in London by Shakbut's younger brother and successor, Zaid, a short time before. Another, more serious one is that the charges made against Shakbut could also be justly applied to most of the rulers who continue to enjoy British patronage in this remote but strategically important part of the world. Not all of them are as rich as Shakbut was, or as miserly, or as determined to prohibit social and economic progress in their countries. But they are as unwilling to reform their feudal and autocratic regimes as he was, and are unaccustomed to spending more than a third of their great unearned wealth for the general benefit of their people.

Playthings for the Sheikhs

The rest of the oil royalties usually go for such playthings as racehorses, motor yachts, new palaces, lavish gifts for local sycophants and distinguished visitors, and of course, fleets of air-conditioned Cadillacs. The royal family of Bahrein, for example, whose income from the American-owned Caltex oil corporation's local subsidiary, Bapco, is comparatively modest—one and a quarter million dollars a month—is said to spend more than twelve million dollars a year on these indulgences. While the sheikhs have built a four-lane highway between the palace and their private beach, many of their 165,000 subjects live in shacks walled and roofed with palm leaves, by the side of sewage-strewn dirt tracks, well traveled by confident giant rats.

Admittedly, most of what money is left over is devoted to the social welfare of the community. Old houses have been converted into hospitals and schools; an agricultural research station has been established; and a few foreign technical experts, medical specialists, and teachers are employed. But the fact that British diplomats hold up Bahrein to the rulers of other states as a model of a progressive monarchy gives an idea of the extent of social deprivation in the area generally.

Saqr, the other sheikh to be dismissed, ruled Sharjah, a still more primitive country where oil has yet to be discovered and whose people are mostly Bedouins. Sharjah is a sizable tract of desert containing a ramshackle palace, a Royal Air Force base, and very little else. Last summer after reigning there for fourteen years, Saqr was quietly bundled aboard an RAF plane and delivered in Egypt as an unexpected guest of President Nasser's government. Since then, he has been addressing a stream of anti-imperialist speeches to his ex-subjects through Radio Cairo.

As a ruler, Saqr showed far more interest in the poems which he wrote laboriously in classical Arabic and had published at his own expense than he did in politics. Toward the end of his reign, when he at last began to pay some attention to the problem of national development, it was too late. His neighbor Sheikh Rashid of Dubai had already laid his hands on most of the capital locally available, and used it to establish a virtual regional trade monopoly, profiting mostly from the smuggling of gold to India, Iran, and, via the latter, the Soviet Union.

With the recklessness of a long-time reader and writer of Arabian romances, Sheikh Saqr decided to take on the British single-handed. He announced that he had accepted an offer of aid from the anti-British Arab League. A few days later, the British Political Residency solemnly stated that he had been overthrown (by his family) on account of his "scandalous behavior and neglect of the welfare of the people."

British Quandary

Thus Britain has been attempting to deal with its quandary in a potentially explosive region where, under an exclusive treaty signed in 1892, it is the only foreign power with the right to diplomatic representation. The quandary is far from unique in diplomatic history, arising as it does from a conflict between a strong desire to maintain the status quo (in this case, to ensure regular supplies of oil) and a realization that the status quo is ultimately unpreservable.

Britain has been involved with the feudal regime of the Persian Gulf for the past 150 years. At the beginning of the nineteenth century, the sheikhs were operating as pirates against passing East India Company ships. A show of force by the Royal Navy in 1820 frightened them sufficiently to sign an agreement to "abstain in perpetuity from acts of piracy and plunder." Some years later, under further duress, they issued proclamations abolishing slavery; and by the end of the century, they had agreed to deal exclusively with Britain.

The discovery of oil in the 1930's came as an unexpected bonus, which Britain's officialdom was slow to grasp. (Many of the best concessions passed into the hands of American companies as a result. Americans now hold about half of all Persian Gulf concessions, with monopolies in four out of nine states, and major prospecting rights in another three; currently they produce 20 per cent of the total oil supply there, and have large stakes in an international consortium producing another 55 per cent.) Large-scale production started after the Second World War, and Britain's dependence on oil supplies from the Persian Gulf had become so great by the 1950's that the blocking of the Suez Canal at the end of 1956 caused stringent gasoline rationing in England.

Instead of striving from then on to diversify its sources of oil, Britain reacted to the emergency by increasing its armed strength in the Persian Gulf area from a few hundred men to more than three thousand. Whitehall [site of British government offices in London] calculated that, having made a makeshift peace with Nasser and got the canal reopened, the primary objective now was to stop the spread of Nasserism to the oil fields themselves.

British diplomats deny any intention of using their dominating position to interfere in the internal affairs of any of the nine kingdoms. But it is a theoretical disclaimer. Any internal revolution would be most unlikely to succeed without some measure of outside support, which could be taken to justify the intervention of British troops.

The diplomats have, at the same time, made efforts to lighten the oppressiveness of the regimes. Their pressure on the rulers has produced at least rudimentary primary education and a few medical services through most of the area. They have prevailed upon Sheikh Mohammed, the illiterate twenty-eight-year-old brother of the ruler of Bahrein who is chief of police, not to arrest political suspects quite so casually and detain them for such long periods without trial, with manacles locked around their ankles which cause festering wounds and scars for life.

Directly after the British removed Sheikh Saqr, they initiated a public works program in Sharjah; and the people of Abu Dhabi can scarcely fail to benefit from the departure of Sheikh Shakbut, who refused to build hospitals and schools, on the grounds that his subjects would not know what to do with them if they had them.

But such activity has delayed, not produced, a solution to the most basic and pressing problem: that the archaic system of government by royalty, evolved within the framework of an isolated, tribal society, is simply unworkable in modern conditions. Apart from its impracticality and its immorality, it is becoming deeply resented by the people who are now living under it.

Oil as a Progressive Force

At the same time that it has brought wealth to the rulers, the discovery of oil has brought a large number of Arabs into contact with Western ideas. The attitudes, particularly toward authority, of American and European oil workers, have made an impression on their Arab employees. The latter are now familiar with such institutions as trade unions, a free press, and universal adult suffrage, although they are denied them. English schoolbooks and Egyptian schoolteachers (whose politics are viewed with suspicion but who are accepted as the only Arabic-speaking teachers that are available) have done much to teach the Gulf Arabs about human rights.

Most communities now have at least one transistor radio, and there is keen local competition between the BBC and Radio Cairo. Although their interpretations of democracy obviously conflict, at least they have made the word a familiar one.

Public relations lobbyists in Beirut, London, and other Western capitals have given the impression that some of the sheikhs are adapting their regimes to fit in with the new aspirations of their subjects. In the area itself, however, there is little evidence of this. Laws are still devised by the rulers personally, in secret consultation with relatives and courtiers, and then proclaimed without further discussion.

Popular representation is held to be unnecessary, on the grounds that any subject has the right of personal appeal to the ruler. Social welfare programs are also said to be superfluous, because anybody in need is supposed to have the right to ask the ruler for help. But the growth of towns—Manama, the capital of Bahrein, has a population of 61,000 and Dubai City one of 55,000—has devalued rights which have been traditional. The sheikhs' regular ostensibly public audiences are deteriorating into mere rituals, slavishly attended by Arab and British officials, partly in the hope of receiving favors and gifts, partly for fear of causing offense. Many genuine petitioners are turned away from the palace doors by the police, and a large number of those who do enter never get to voice their pleas.

Furthermore, young, literate Arabs, whose learning is often greater than their rulers', are no longer willing to go down on their bended knees to request humbly as favors what the radio and books have told them are their rights. The assumption that public property actually belongs to the royal family also causes resentment, particularly when a ruler grandiosely goes through the motions of presenting some of it, usually a piece of land, to the nation and then expects to be praised by a grateful populace for his generosity.

The American and British oil companies have, in fact, demanded and ultimately created for themselves a generation of industrial workers, skilled tradesmen, and merchants. To qualify, the Arabs have had to abandon the tribal loyalties of their fathers and adopt some Western standards. They are cynical about palace corruption, licentiousness (Bahrein is a stopover with a unique reputation among airline hostesses), and unearned opulence, ashamed of the servile traditions of their people toward royalty, and perhaps too uncritical of what they have been told about Egypt, Europe, and the United States; and their privately expressed hostility toward the sheikhs has become much more marked, even in the past year.

Incompetent Rebels

So far, the number of "freedom fighters" in the area is minute, for all the exhortations of Radio Cairo. Their record up to now is one of utter incompetence: their most recent efforts have been to blow up a water main in the mistaken belief that it was an oil pipeline, and to try to set fire to a sealed storage tank of crude oil by lighting an old newspaper underneath it.

If not their methods, their cause is supported by most of the rest of the Arab world, and it is becoming popular in the Persian Gulf area itself. The sheikhs have refused to convert their feudal regimes into constitutional democracies and to become mere figureheads. The British are too timid, despite the strength of their position, to do any more than arrange for the removal of the worst and least cooperative of the sheikhs, and substitute slightly better ones.

. . . [As] British troops are withdrawn from Aden . . . [before 1970] as Harold Wilson has promised they will be, Britain's position in the Persian Gulf area will become still more entrenched. The Middle East Command Headquarters is to be moved to Bahrein (just eight years after it was moved to Aden from Cyprus), and the base in Sharjah is already being enlarged.

British diplomats are trying hard to play down the significance of this change, and to persuade British newspapers to do likewise. It is claimed that the increase in military personnel in Bahrein will be "hardly noticeable" and that there is no danger of the island's developing into a "second Aden." But as recent events in Aden have been, in many respects, a repetition of the history of Cyprus (which Britain was determined never to repeat), it is not easy to feel much confidence in the ability of British diplomats to learn from past mistakes.

FERMENT IN IRAQ [6]

When night falls beside the Tigris River, Abu Nawas Street awakes.

Lights shine above the little tables where men play backgammon in open-air casinos. Brushwood fires roast spitted river fish for the diners in riverside restaurants. The moon lights the placid river and the ancient city appears at peace.

Baghdad's calm on these hot nights is deceptive. Beneath it lies a sense of near explosion. The comments a visitor hears—their authors cannot be identified in a society that appears increasingly repressive—tell of a ferment of unrest in the capital and in the countryside, of economic, political and religious strains that seem to be slowly shredding the nation's fabric.

[6] From "Intense Economic and Political Strains Beset Iraq," by Drew Middleton, staff correspondent. New York *Times.* p 2. My. 15, '68. © 1968 by The New York Times Company. Reprinted by permission.

Discontent infects almost every important group in Iraq's 8.25 million people—the students, the middle class, the unions and the army....

There are many causes for unrest in Iraq: frustration over a potentially rich country's laggard economic development, growing opposition to continuing rule by presidential decree, bitterness among militant Arab elements because President Abdel Rahman Arif refuses to follow the path set by President Gamal Abdel Nasser of the United Arab Republic, the strain imposed on the patriarchical society of the desert and the farms by rapid economic and political change.

In scores of hurried, furtive conversations, no one could guess when an explosion might come, but there are abundant signs that the Iraqis are stretched close to the breaking point.

The government, usually considered the most conservative of those classed as revolutionary in this part of the world, says little. Requests for talks with ministers and officials go unanswered. But the voices of the restive and the aggrieved are seldom silent.

Common Goal of Many

A demand for the restoration of constitutional parliamentary government is the common goal of many of the discontented. President Arif's recent promise to hold elections in two years and to establish a provisional legislature did little to quiet those who oppose government by decree, the extension of which was attributed to the general Middle Eastern situation.

The demand for parliamentary government has economic as well as political roots. The discontented do not believe that a provisional legislature picked by the president will goad the government into the action needed to accelerate progress.

A student scoffed: "Promises, they'll do nothing and in two years they'll find another reason to postpone elections again."

And a businessman said:

As long as there is no parliament, no real political parties, no free press, the government does as it likes. They put money into arms instead of development. They worry about Israel instead of Iraq.

We could be as prosperous as Iran [he added]. We have oil, good land. We have everything but a government that will act.

The Soviet Union benefits most from this unrest. With the United States unrepresented here—relations were broken during the Arab-Israeli war last June—Soviet diplomats and propagandists have had a clear field among the discontented. They reinforced their presence by a visit here today by two Soviet naval vessels touring the Middle East.

Educators said youth generally had reacted positively to Soviet propaganda, which has recently been reinforced by the return of the first Iraqi graduates of Soviet universities. The government-controlled press hymns the glories of the Communist way of life in articles whose topics range from boxing to chemistry.

Yet a residue of respect for Western institutions remains, especially among the more outspoken members of the middle class. Even a student who had plumped for collectivization of agriculture argued vehemently for the restoration of parliament.

Students Are Restive

The students, particularly those of Baghdad University, are one of the four main centers of unrest. The Baghdad students, who struck last winter, talk of another strike or demonstrations for free institutions and greater economic opportunity.

The trade unions have become increasingly discontented. Their members charge that the government has frozen wages outside the oil industry and has added useless workers to payrolls. This cuts unemployment but reduces productivity. . . . [A] union member said, "They even closed down our newspaper when they closed the privately owned papers."

Land reform, nationalization, punitive taxation and re-strictive regulations have whittled away the influence of the middle class in the ten years since a revolutionary mob killed the youthful King Faisal and Nuri as-Said, his premier.

One businessman will have to pay 74 per cent more tax as a result of new amendments to the income-tax law. A former minister of the crown almost tearfully implores old friends to employ his daughter as a typist.

Said a professional man: "If I could leave, I would, but I cannot, so we will wait. Something must happen. We can-not blunder along like this."

Finally, there is the army, which put President Arif's brother, Abdel Salem, in power in 1963—he died in a heli-copter crash in 1966—and keeps his successor there. The army, despite the increasingly close ties with the Soviet Union, still shows strong leanings toward the West and fears Soviet influence as a threat to its independence.

The president removed four senior generals in February and, at the moment, is seeking to consolidate his position by wooing junior officers.

The Palestine Liberation Organization maintains a re-cruiting office in Baghdad and teams tour the universities raising money for the resistance struggle against Israel. But Iraq's involvement in the conflict seems less pervasive than that of Jordan or the United Arab Republic.

President Arif told an Arab interviewer recently that it was imperative to intensify and unite the guerrilla resistance to Israel. He wants an Arab summit meeting to agree on a "unified plan" of action and concurs with the Arab leaders' stand that there be "no peace and no negotiations with Is-rael."

Shift of Focus Discerned

Despite such ritualistic statements and the stationing of 10,000 Iraqi troops in Jordan as a gesture of support, the government here gives signs of being aware that the economic situation and the constitutional issue are more important to the people than the conflict with Israel.

Many people contend that defense is built up at the expense of economic development, particularly in agriculture. The production of wheat and barley has decreased steadily since land reform. The government's problem is that it cannot risk offending the army, which was placated with the purchase of new weapons from France.

Iraq's pressing new problems are superimposed on old ones. The Shiite sect of Islam, which resents a government largely composed of more Orthodox Sunni Muslims, is increasingly active in underground politics. There are signs that it intends to make common cause with the Kurds in the north.

Kurds Are Fearful

The Kurds fear that the arms purchased in France will be used to deprive them of their hard-won autonomy and not against Israel.

Publication of the Kurdish newspaper *Al Taakhi* was recently suspended for thirty days. The government said the suspension was because the newspaper's views were "prejudicial to national unity." The action followed publication of an article bitterly critical of the regime's political and economic policies.

Thoughtful Iraqis believe the troubled present is not susceptible to easy solution. They see their nation instinctively rejecting both communism and capitalism but unable to find its own path. Meanwhile, the glib whisperers in the tea houses and casinos can always win an audience by blaming Iraq's woes on the American imperialists and their Israeli "puppets."

THE ARAB DELUSION [7]

"Maalesh! Inshallah!"

Anyone who knows the Arabs would immediately recognize these terms. To the non-Arab they cause uncertainty, frustration, often bewilderment. To the Arab they offer comfort, hope, relief in affliction. It is not difficult to translate these terms into English, but impossible to convey their exact meaning. *Maalesh!*—sorry! it doesn't matter! it'll be all right! A charming term, it stands for the immense tolerance the Arabs have, indicates also the submissiveness, the apathy and the negativism of the Arabs. *Inshallah!*—God willing—represents the fatalism, the wishful thinking, and the inability of the Arabs to face reality. It is understandable to have faith in God, but it is fatal not to be able to take responsibility. "We lost a war, *Maalesh! Inshallah,* we will win next time! . . ."

It is difficult to think of another people who have deceived themselves in the way we Arabs have. Fantasy, lying, wishful thinking and false pride substitute for rational thinking in the Arab mind. We prefer to believe that basically nothing is wrong with our way of life, beliefs, or social values. We look to our ancient past for our glory and ignore a millennium of servitude, corruption and submission as if it did not have any impact on our values, social behavior, and ideology. It is incredible how little is understood about Arab history. There is no comprehensive study of Arab history in Arabic. There are only translations of outdated Western works or paraphrasings of these works without acknowledgment to the original authors. Students of Arab history are painfully aware of the absence of an adequate comprehensive study in any language.

Both Western and Arab intellectuals see the dynamic force of Islam as shaping early Arab history. Both agree on

[7] From "Maalesh! Inshallah!" by M. A. Shaban, lecturer at the University of London's School of Oriental and African Studies. *Encounter* (London). 30: 37-9. F. '68. Reprinted by permission.

the immense Islamic heritage the Arabs passed on to humanity. But while most Western intellectuals argue that Islam is a spent force or is in need of a reformation, Arabs refuse to recognize the weaknesses which have crept into their Islamic heritage. Confronted with the challenge of the West, Arabs thought that they had only to learn the "secret" of Western progress to catch up with the West and rid themselves of Western domination. We must only add Western technology to our cherished heritage and everything would straighten itself out. Arab socialism, Westernization, modernization and Arab nationalism are among the empty slogans which have been used by Arabs recently to hide our inability to face our weaknesses. We do not want to admit that Arab society has undergone a long period of deformation which has badly damaged the fundamental values as well as the social and intellectual life of every Arab. . . .

Contact with the West impressed nineteenth century Arab intellectuals, but the transgressions of Western colonialism left a feeling of mistrust in the mind of every Arab. When Pan-Islamism was involved against Western imperialism, it proved ineffective. Yet, ironically, liberal nationalism (in itself a Western notion) proved to be effective in Egypt, Syria, and even Algeria, and helped in the struggle against Western domination. But it has proved inadequate to reform a deformed society. It is true the Arabs have become free to shape their own future. But the persistence of the West in its attempts to maintain its influence in the Middle East was bound to interfere with Arab efforts in this respect. Western policies—e.g., Suez, 1956—have been disastrous for the region and have increased immeasurably mistrust of the West and all it stands for.

Islam and Westernism

A new factor has of late been introduced into the situation. A few Arab intellectuals had begun to toy with ideas of socialism and communism, but until the early 1950's socialism remained mostly a dirty word in the Arab world. It was not so much that communism and Islam are incompatible as that the Arab was ignorant of communism. This long-imposed ignorance, combined with the sudden introduction of socialist ideas (and, of course, the Soviet attitude towards the Arabs), helped to remove the fear of communism from the mind of the Arab intellectual. Still, he is not ready yet to accept a Communist ideology.

In this frame of mind the Arab intellectual is faced by a new challenge, namely Zionism, with its peculiar amalgam of Westernism, socialism, and nationalism based on racial and religious foundations. The Jews have succeeded where the Arabs failed. They have succeeded in reviving an antiquated religion whose adherents had suffered in complete submissiveness over the centuries. Since the Israeli idea was conceived by Western Jews, it was easier for them to adopt Western values. A vigorous and dynamic society succeeded in imposing itself on Palestine in spite of continued Arab objection.

In the absence of an indigenous philosophy the alternatives for the Arabs are clear. There are those who advocate communism, and they have a powerful argument in the support of Russia for the Arab cause. They also cite the achievements of communism in China. Nevertheless, they know they are only a small minority and they lack the organization to accomplish their objectives; they also believe that the Arab world may drift inadvertently into communism, and they calculate that time is on their side. Of course this *could* happen—in Syria to begin with and perhaps also in Egypt. The pressures of the present situation may push in this direction.

The West has a responsibility and a chance to help the Arabs out of their present dilemma. It must surely realize that the Arabs are anti-Communist. It is the Communists who are supporting the Arabs and not the other way round. The Arabs are against the West's world-politics, but they are not against Western values. If the West would try simply not to offend the Arabs—let alone right the wrongs it has committed against them—the Arabs might regain their faith in the West and its values. The Arabs need to realize that they should accept Western values even if they contradict the Islamic heritage. Islam should be relegated completely to the relationship of man to God.

The West needs to realize that it is never too late to right a wrong, and the more candidly this is done the sooner forgotten. The Jews have almost forgotten the wrongs inflicted on them in the Christian West over the centuries. One reads about a Judaeo-Christian tradition. Could one hope for a Judaeo-Christian-Muslim tradition? Or should one expect Arab communism? Almost anything would be better than the immemorial *Maalesh! Inshallah!*

II. BACKGROUND TO THE ARAB-ISRAELI WAR

EDITOR'S INTRODUCTION

The focus of this volume is necessarily the Arab-Israeli conflict of 1967 and its aftermath. In the two articles that follow, John Badeau and Barbara Tuchman evaluate the war within the over-all historical and political context of the two cultures. From the Arabs, nurturing a feeling of injustice that dates from the end of World War II when the Western powers split up the Ottoman Empire, came a series of apparent miscalculations as to the capacity and readiness of the Israelis to wage war. The Arab penchant for rhetoric not merely as a substitute for action but as a form of action itself led the Arabs into risking more than they bargained for.

The Israelis, too, may have miscalculated. The swiftness of their victory, their diplomatic isolation, and the responsibility for administering large occupied territories—all this has caused Israel to reevaluate her own position in the Middle East. By insisting that the Arabs negotiate a peace treaty directly with Israel (when there is little sign that the Arabs are prepared to yield to these conditions), the Israelis now find themselves in the awkward position of an occupying power. For the Arabs, "to wait is to win." The fact that Israel is saddled with the administration of extensive territories may not trouble the Arabs in the way that Tel Aviv expected. Since the Arabs do not, in the Israeli view, "act in their own best interests," Israel may be forced to readjust her own policy toward her neighbors. Within Israel the debate goes on as to whether these occupied lands should not form part of a Greater Israel. Yet to accept this solution would be to incur increased Arab enmity. From this perspective, it is hard not to believe that time works for rather than against Arab revanchism.

THE ARABS, 1967 [1]

As the dust of battle settled over Sinai after six brief days
of fighting, only the spoor of fleeing Arab forces remained to
mark the tragic Arab-Israeli conflict of June 1967. Yet though
the victory was swift and irrevocable, it has not yet proved
decisive. Will stunning defeat bring the Arabs to their moment of truth, marking the beginning of the end of their
hostility toward Israel? Or may it be the end of the beginning
of Israel's existence, ushering in a Hundred Years' War in
which the rising tide of Arab population and resources ultimately will engulf the tiny state? These questions cannot
now be answered; much will depend upon the accuracy and
realism with which the causes of the recent struggle are ap-
praised and their lessons applied to the future.

In the immediate aftermath of conflict, there has been a
tendency to oversimplify and emotionalize the issues, re-
ducing them to terms of innocence and blame which absolve
each party from responsibility in its own eyes. To both sides
and their supporters, the key lies in "aggression," that port-
manteau word which modern man must eschew since it is not
respectable to admit anything but "defensive" military action. Thus the Arabs claim their action was "defensive"
since (they maintain) Israel fired the shot and launched the
invasion which precipitated war. Israel points to the closing
of the Gulf of Aqaba as the *casus belli,* to which their military action was only a defensive response. Which was the
true cause for the outbreak of war?

The answer must be that neither was; what broke out in
overt conflict was the surfacing of disputes and policies to
which each contestant had long contributed. On their part,
the Arabs had persistently underestimated the reality and
predictability of Israel's reaction to nineteen years of unre-

[1] Article by John S. Badeau, for seventeen years variously a professor, dean,
and president at the American University in Cairo; former American Ambassador to the United Arab Republic; presently director of the Middle East Institute
at Columbia University. *Atlantic.* 220:102-4+. D. '67. Copyright © by the author.
Reprinted by permission.

lenting hostility by the encircling Arab world. Faced with a sustained state of belligerency, the target of constant threats and innuendoes, beset with intermittent border raids and terrorist attacks, Israel could not be counted upon to exercise restraint under mounting provocation—as any perceptive Arab leader should have known. No state can acquiesce in a permanent threat to its existence, no government can abdicate its responsibility to protect the lives and property of its citizens from attack. Sustained periods of guerrilla terrorism, such as that which began in the summer of 1966, would inevitably generate a sharp Israeli reaction, and the Arabs have only themselves to blame if they failed to recognize this.

That they consistently underestimated the temper of Israel is due in part to the difference between the credibility of Arab and Israeli statements of intent. The Arab world is highly verbal; words are often ends in themselves and not necessarily forerunners of action. The fact that an Arab leader states a purpose publicly is not an invariable sign that he will carry it out, as the shrill crescendo of verbal inter-Arab warfare during the past few years clearly shows. Too often the Arabs tended to give the same weight to Israeli statements that they gave to their own, to their dismay when prompt action followed.

Moreover, Arab estimates of Israeli intentions were affected by their conviction that the great powers (especially the United States) really controlled the country; hence Israel would not make a major move without foreign support and acquiescence, if not with actual urging. The possibility of Israeli armed action thus went beyond what Israel itself might purpose and be capable of doing, involving estimates of what the West would allow Israel to do. The immediate and universal Arab acceptance of the fiction that American planes assisted Israel in its attack against the U.A.R. [United Arab Republic, i.e. Egypt] was due in part to the belief that Israel could not have undertaken military action without the encouragement and support of the United States—hence it appeared credible that American planes were dispatched to help Israel. This seemed the more logical in view of the long history of American commitments and arms sales to Israel, and the flood of public statements across the years from leading American personalities and politicians giving uncritical support to Israel's cause.

Deep Are the Roots

But the Arab action which led to the 1967 conflict had deeper roots. The reasons for sustained Arab hostility toward Israel are more profound and intricate than many Americans allow themselves to believe. Such simple answers as "Arabs hate Jews," "the backward Arab world fears the existence of a modern and democratic state in its midst," "the Arabs in general do not feel deeply about Israel, it is their leaders who whip up enmity for their own purposes" not only explain nothing, but are untrue. Such shallow estimates of Arab motivation have led many supporters of Israel to underestimate the depth and stamina of the Arab response and to be oversanguine that a determined display of force will lead to peace. The question is not one of accepting the Arab point of view, but of understanding it, so that approaches and policies will be grounded in realism and not in wishful thinking. If the Arabs have persistently, and to their hurt, underestimated the fact of Israel's existence and its predictable response to their enmity, Israel and its supporters have as persistently, and to their hurt, underestimated the facts of Arab feelings and the problems Israel's existence poses for them.

The outbreak of conflict in the spring of 1967, after nine years of relative peace, encapsuled the principal elements in the Arab attitude toward Israel. Its most basic lesson is that Arab hostility is still bitter and ubiquitous after nearly two decades of fruitless struggle. In many ways, 1967 was not a repetition of 1956, when the Egyptian response to Israel's invasion of its territory was a limited action and did not precipitate general Arab war. It was rather a return to 1948, when the Arabs fought as a group against the existence of Israel as a country. It is this fact which has baffled and angered so many who support Israel. They feel it is irrational and irresponsible for a people to continue hostility so long and in the face of such repeated failure. By this time the Arabs should have made their peace with events and come to terms with what they could not undo. That they have not done so, the argument runs, must be due to an irrational streak in their temperament, to the cynical machinations of their leaders, to irradicable anti-Jewism, or to the scheming of the Soviet Union.

Yet of all people, the Jewish community should understand the tenacity of racial memory and long-sustained feeling. Through the years of dispersion, they never forgot Palestine, although it was only since the last century that this steadfastness involved dedication to the re-creation of a Jewish state in the long-remembered homeland.

This is not to say that the factors involved in the Jewish attachment to Israel are precisely the same as those contained in the Arab sense of connection with Palestine. Palestine was not the original historical center of life and religion for the Arabs, as it was for Jewry. The Arabs were not a minority dispersed through many lands, and they did not suffer under discrimination and persecution, as many Jews had. They never faced a threat of racial extinction, as European Jews did under Nazism, in which a national refuge became a matter of life and death for many. Although Palestine had been an Arab land since at least the seventh century and contained important religious sites (both Christian and Muslim), it did not fill the horizon of Arab consciousness, as it did for many Jews. Why then is the Arab connection with Palestine so strong and the sense of outrage at its loss so deep?

The most basic cause is found in the intense Arab reaction against long-continued domination of their destinies by foreign countries. In the fading days of Ottoman rule, the Arab communities of the Middle East were stirred by nationalistic consciousness akin to that involved in the emergence of the Zionist ideal in Jewry. They sought cultural revival, political expression, and community selfhood within the body of the Turkish Empire—a recognition of "Arabistan" as an entity in which the destiny of the Arab people could be achieved. Thwarted in their struggle, some of their principal leaders responded to British promises during the First World War and joined the Allies in the overthrow of Ottoman rule. They did so on the understanding that their national aspirations would be recognized and some form of independent Arab rule achieved.

In recent days there have been repeated references to the statement of Faisal (a principal leader of the Arab Revolt in 1916-1918 and later King of Iraq) that there was no conflict between the aims of Zionism and Arab nationalism. Those who quote it leave out the essential condition which Faisal attached to his statement, that *all the promises made to the Arabs should be fulfilled.* This was not done; the attempt to create an Arab state was checkmated by France and Great Britain, who carved up the Arab portion of the defunct Ottoman Empire to suit their own purposes. The creation of Iraq, Syria, modern Lebanon, Jordan, and (mandated) Palestine was not a fulfillment of Arab independence, but the parceling out of Arab populations to suit the convenience of the victorious Allied powers.

The Great Betrayal

The Arabs never forgot this. It was the great betrayal of their national cause, the incontestable proof that the West meant to divide and rule them in its own interests. After two decades of sharp struggle between individual nationalisms in Arab countries and their Western masters, the Second World War came to erode imperial ties and create a new organ of international action. Arab nationalism took new hope and looked forward to becoming at last the master of its own destiny.

It was at this juncture that the creation of Israel was forced on the Arab world. The plea that Nazi persecution justified the creation did not move the Arabs, since these persecutions were the product of anti-Semitism in the Western world and not in the Middle East, where Arab-Jewish relations had been remarkably good. "It was the West which persecuted the Jews," said the Arabs; "now they want to get rid of their problem by pushing it off on us and using our land."

But the Arabs did not see Israel simply as a device of the West to rid itself of an unconscionable problem at the expense of another people. It was for them a tactic of fading imperial power to continue its control of Arab destinies. The position of the British in Arab lands was rapidly and irrevocably fading; now they sought to bolster up their weakness by creating Israel as a Western bridgehead, confronting the Arab world with a situation which would trouble and divide it. In the ensuing attack on the new state, the Arabs were not so much responding to the existence of Israel per se as to a long history of foreign control, domination, and manipulation at the hands of the great powers. Israel became, and has remained, the symbol of the Arab national struggle against foreign control.

This reaction was not merely a psychological fact of the Arab mind; it stemmed from and was given content by the process through which Israel came into being. The United Nations did not consult the wishes of the majority community in Palestine (the Arabs were nearly two thirds of the population) in regard to their political future. On the basis of Jewish ownership of some 23 per cent of the total cultivatable land area of the country, Israel was given nearly 40 per cent of Palestine. The vote in the United Nations which created the state came only after long debate and was due in part (the Arabs allege, with some justification) to the Western bloc and the pressure it was able to mount on client states. The Arabs have always maintained that the United Nations did not have the authority under its charter to dispose of their territory, especially without regard to the wishes of the inhabitants. They can only see that Israel was rammed down their throats by the same forces which so long had manipulated their national life.

Perhaps the Arabs should forget all this after nineteen years of fruitless struggle and recognize that history seldom moves to right past wrongs; but they have not, and they will not. After all, two decades is a short span in the thirteen centuries of Arab history; Palestine has been lost to the Arabs before and ultimately regained—it could happen again. The inherent superiority of Arab resources (presently thirty times the population of Israel and eight times its gross national product), the growing modernization of Arab life, the rising power of the non-Western world in international affairs, and the legitimacy of their aspirations make the Arabs feel that time is on their side more than it is on Israel's.

Moreover, the Arabs read Israel's policies since its founding as proof that it intends to be a law unto itself, not bound by the international community to which it owes its existence. On the eve of the creation of the new state, the Zionist radical underground launched a series of unprovoked attacks on certain Arab territories to force their inclusion within Israel, although they did not lie within the borders created by the United Nations resolution—a fact which has been acknowledged with some gratitude by Israeli leaders. In recent years, Israel has been deliberately uncooperative with the United Nations Mixed Armistice Commission, refusing to participate in many of its meetings. After the 1956 attack on Egypt, Israel categorically refused the United Nations' request to station a new peacekeeping force (UNEF) on its soil, although Egypt accepted for its own territory in the Gaza Strip. The demilitarized zones, created by the Armistice Agreement which ended the 1948 fighting, have been a cause of continuing dispute. Repeatedly Israel has attempted to extend agriculture and land reclamation into these areas, over the Arab insistence that this violated their status quo under the agreement. This was one reason for the intermittent clashes along the Syrian border which led to the 1966-1967 Syrian hostility. In Arab eyes, this record gave the image of an aggressive Israel, only accepting United Nations controls and operations when they served its own purposes.

The Refugee Problem

This image was sharpened by the one problem which, more than any other aspect of the existence of Israel, has stirred Arab resentment and fanned the embers of Arab hostility—the plight of the Arab refugee. As a result of the founding of Israel, over one million Arab inhabitants of Palestine became refugees in neighboring countries. Nearly a quarter of the original refugee group fled their country before the British forces were withdrawn and Israel came into being. The remaining three quarters were uprooted during the hostilities and the period when the cease-fire was being negotiated. One of the first actions of the United Nations after the 1948 conflict was to call for the return of these refugees to their homes; on December 11, 1948, the General Assembly adopted a resolution stating "that refugees wishing to return to their homes and live at peace with their neighbors should be permitted to do so at the earliest practical date, and that compensation should be paid for the property of those choosing not to return and for the loss and damage to property."

This resolution was repeatedly reaffirmed, yet Israel did not take steps to implement it, the Israeli view being that it would discuss the refugee problem only in the context of a general peace settlement. The Arabs have maintained that the right of people to return to and reside on their own property is a basic human right, not subject to collateral conditions, and cite the UN resolution in defense of this.

Israel and some of its supporters have countered this claim by maintaining that the refugees left voluntarily, being lured from their homes by provocative Arab broadcasts which promised that they would return in triumph once victory had been won. There is no dependable historical evidence that this counterclaim was true; tapes allegedly recording such broadcasts have been cited, but never produced for impartial inspection. The fact is that most of the refugees fled because they were afraid, afraid of being caught between the lines of battle, afraid of terrorist raids by the Zionist underground such as that which destroyed the village of Dar Yassin on April 9, 1948, in which some 250 unarmed Arabs were massacred. Yet, regardless of the reasons for flight, the Arabs (and apparently the United Nations) have taken the view that a man has a right to return to his home no matter what the reason for his leaving—so long (as the UN resolution stated) as he intends to live peacefully with his neighbors.

This tragic situation has left in the heart of the Arab world a mass of dislocated and bitter people, dependent on international charity for their existence, taxing the resources of the countries to which they have fled, and nursing a deep sense of grievance against those who now occupy their homes. Movements like the Palestine Liberation Organization and leaders like Ahmed Shukairy are not due so much to the calculated policy of Arab states as to the festering sore of the refugee camps. The failure of Israel to show any concern for this problem, to make any serious attempt to carry out the United Nations resolution, or even to admit a responsibility toward the refugees which it could not presently implement because of its own security problem is read by the Arabs as proof that Israel is basically anti-Arab.

Admittedly, these Arab views of Israel are partial, emotional, not taking into account Israel's own problems and the problem Israel itself was created to solve. The dispassionate political analyst will not read the situation either as the Arab or as the Israeli does. Both Arab and Israeli motives are mixed, and both highlight the factors which favor their cause and neglect those which weaken it. But Arab feelings are genuine, deep, founded upon a case which cannot be summarily dismissed as simply irrational hatred or political maneuver. This case and the feelings it engenders are a fundamental cause of the 1967 conflict; without taking full account of them, any explanation of Arab actions is partial and misleading.

Lessons from Experience

It is still too early to establish a definitive account of all that transpired in precipitating the outbreak of hostilities in June 1967, but there are certain general factors affecting the Arab action which are clear. One was the continuing effect on Egypt and the Arab world of the 1956 Israeli invasion of Egypt. Because this was followed by ten years of relative (if uneasy) calm, it has largely been forgotten in the West, but Egypt and President Nasser did not forget it. From that bitter experience, the military and political leadership of Egypt drew three conclusions.

The first was that Israel would "try it again" when a propitious opportunity for military action offered itself. In the winter and spring of 1967, the U.A.R. and Syria believed they had evidence that Israel might be preparing for another round. In response to continued border raids, Premier Eshkol gave public warning in the Knesset that Israel might take drastic action, hinting at a military retaliation against Syria. This warning was given unusual weight by the Syrians and Egyptians because of the Israeli punitive action against the Jordanian village of el Sammu in November, 1956. To Eshkol's warning was added the fact that at the annual parade in Jerusalem on Israel's Independence Day, some heavy military equipment was conspicuously absent—could it be massed on the borders of Syria for an attack? The suspicion was confirmed when the Soviets apparently reported to the Syrians in late April or early May that their intelligence had detected an Israeli armed concentration on the Syrian border. It is not possible to know whether this was a complete fabrication or rested upon some hard evidence; the important thing is that it confirmed Syrian and Egyptian fears. Shortly thereafter both the Syrian and Egyptian intelligence claimed that they had independent confirmation of the Soviet report.

Many will scoff at the idea that Israel was preparing to repeat its 1956 maneuver, or had any aggressive intent toward its neighboring Arab states. What is important is not the fact, but the belief in Syrian and Egyptian minds. Given the experience of a sudden Israeli attack eleven years earlier, which obviously had been well planned, it is not surprising that the Arabs were prepared to believe the worst. This belief did not concern Israel alone; it also included Arab estimates of Western policy. In 1956 Israel had been aided and abetted by France and Great Britain, the full story of whose complicity is just beginning to be revealed.

In 1967 it seemed to the Egyptians that Great Britain and the United States might be urging Israel on in its alleged aggressive policies. Britain and the U.A.R. had long been involved in a confrontation in South Arabia, where Egypt was supporting the most radical wing of the Aden national struggle. American-Egyptian relations had steadily deteriorated since 1965; American aid to the U.A.R. had virtually ceased, and by the winter of 1967 President Nasser believed that the United States had written off the U.A.R. in its Arab policies and was determined to undermine his position. On several occasions he and other senior members of his government expressed the conviction that a "confrontation" between the two countries was inevitable. Given the American connection with Israel and the memory of the carefully concealed Anglo-French involvement in the 1956 affair, it seemed plausible that behind Israel's disquieting statements and (reported) military movements lay Anglo-American conniving.

A second lesson drawn from the 1956 experience was that never again could Egypt afford to be caught with its armed forces unmobilized in the face of a possible invasion. The 1956 attack caught the Egyptian Army completely unprepared—although the crescendo of border incidents should have warned them of the possibility of a major Israeli response. Defeated once by unpreparedness (as they saw it), they would not run the risk of a second experience. The development of the Egyptian Army after 1956, with its better training and larger supply of advanced weapons, gave confidence that if the army were in position, it could prevent an aggressive action, perhaps even carry war into Israeli territory. At the same time, mobilization would serve to warn Israel and those allegedly behind it that the U.A.R. was on to the game and would not be caught napping this time.

But in mobilizing, it is doubtful that the U.A.R. felt it ran too great a risk of actual conflict, for the third lesson it drew from 1956 was that the world community would not allow another war between Israel and the Arabs. President Nasser freely expressed this conviction on a number of occasions, saying that since the world community had stopped Israel in its attack against the Arabs in 1956, it would also stop an Arab attack against Israel, giving this as one reason why he opposed plans for a general Arab-Israeli war.

Despite the usual flood of bellicose statements, it does not appear on the basis of information now available that the U.A.R. was planning to attack Israel out of hand. It seems rather to have responded to what it considered the possibility of Israeli action by taking the step of complete and challenging mobilization on Israel's borders, believing that it could do so with safety on the basis of its own military strength and the probability that international forces would restrain Israel and find some way out of the situation short of war.

It may be argued that President Nasser's request for the withdrawal of UNEF from the Gaza Strip makes this view invalid, his true object being to get the United Nations out of the way so that he *could* attack Israel. No conclusive judgment can yet be given on this, but there is evidence which suggests that the U.A.R. did not expect or plan for the complete dismounting of the UN peacekeeping operation. From his standpoint, Secretary-General U Thant acted correctly; no UN peace force could remain on the soil of a host country over that country's objection. Moreover, it seems to have been the Secretary-General's conviction that unless a peacekeeping force had full freedom to exercise its function, it must be withdrawn, both to protect the UN from blame of ineffectiveness for which it was not responsible, and to secure freedom for future peacekeeping operations in other situations. Additionally, Yugoslavia and India appeared to be considering the withdrawal of their contingents from UNEF.

Despite these conditions and the logic they imposed on the situation, it appears that the U.A.R. was taken by surprise by the instant and complete dispersal of UNEF. Apparently President Nasser expected that the observers would be withdrawn from the borders to Gaza, then the matter carried back to the UN with delaying diplomatic tactics which might result in some compromise solution.

That this did not happen seems to have been an important element in the outbreak of conflict. Once the UNEF force was withdrawn from the Strait of Tiran, the Egyptian Army naturally replaced it. In Egyptian eyes this returned the Gulf of Aqaba to its pre-1956 position. The chief gain Israel had made from 1956 was the opening of the Gulf of Aqaba, which became the symbol to the Egyptians of their defeat and the unwarranted "fruit of aggression" on the part of Israel. The temptation was too strong to be resisted. Encouraged by plaudits from the Arab world, Nasser moved to erase the last blot from the Egyptian scutcheon and return his country's sovereignty over its own territory to what it had been before the Israeli attack in 1956.

Miscalculations

In all this it is clear that the Egyptians were badly misled when they asumed that the world of 1967 was so like the world of 1956 that hostilities would be prevented by international action. American-Soviet cooperation was not possible, as it had been eleven years earlier. The Soviets were under pressure from their dispute with China and at odds with the United States over Vietnam. The problems of the NATO alliance, with the defection of France and the weakening of the British position, made united Western action highly improbable—as American failure to rally support against the closing of the Gulf of Aqaba showed. Israel had strengthened its political and foreign policy self-determination and had increased its military power. 1967 was not 1956, and it was a calamitous miscalculation to assume that Arabs could confront Israel with impunity behind the shield of an expected international intervention.

While the memory of 1956 and the lessons the Arabs drew from it formed the general framework for their actions in 1967, there were at least two other important factors involved. The first was the relationship between the U.A.R. and Syria. After the dissolution of the Egyptian-Syrian union in 1961, the two countries entered a period of intermittent cold war and revolutionary rivalry. Syria has always felt that it was the wellspring of Arab unity, and its Baath Party saw itself as the original and true delineator of Arab socialism. Nasser's claims to Arab leadership and socialist pioneering did not sit well with the Syrians, who resented what had happened to them under the United Arab Republic. Part of Syria's proprietary sense of Arab unity was expressed by its uncompromising stand against Israel; of all Arab countries, Syria was the most consistently provocative in its Israeli policies.

Syria was a problem to the U.A.R. Its stand against Israel could not be openly repudiated, nor its claim to revolutionary socialism written off. After some five years of tension, the U.A.R. moved (partly under Soviet prodding) to plaster over its differences with Syria, and in the fall of 1966, entered into a defensive alliance with Damascus. On the surface this appeared to be a move against Israel, but in fact it was partly a device through which the U.A.R. hoped to restrain Syrian adventures which might embroil the U.A.R. in an unplanned and undesired conflict. This objective was also present in the earlier formation of the Unified Military Command, a device by which the U.A.R. hoped to have some influence in the military planning of other Arab states as a partial guarantee against their unilateral action.

During the growing tension between Syria and Israel in the winter of 1967, the U.A.R. was relatively quiet, but after the major air battle in the early spring, when the Syrians were badly defeated, Syria pressed the U.A.R. to honor its commitment. Credibility is as important to the U.A.R. as it is to the United States, and Nasser either had to repudiate his undertaking or to fulfill it. Given the circumstance already described, and certain special Egyptian problems presently to be discussed, the U.A.R. threw in its lot with Syria, and to a measure, became a captive of that country's aggressive anti-Israel policies. That Nasser did this was due in part to his conviction that the U.A.R. military establishment could stand up against Israel should conflict break out.

This is only one illustration of how the Palestine problem has been a continuing factor in inter-Arab politics. This is the one issue on which no Arab leader can turn his back without risking his position, either in his own country or in the Arab world. Bourguiba was able to take a soft line toward Israel without imperiling his domestic position, but he paid for it by losing influence among his Arab neighbors.

This leads to the second factor in U.A.R. actions other than the impact of 1956—the particular problems Egypt was facing in its relations with the Arab world. After the Syrian defection in 1961 and President Nasser's growing stalemate in Yemen, Egyptian reputation steadily eroded. King Faisal's adroit diplomacy checkmated the U.A.R. on a number of occasions, the Unified Military Command, which Egypt had sponsored, began to break up, divisions within the Arab League were so sharp that it was impossible to hold a proposed chief-of-states conference to consider common Arab problems. Thus the U.A.R. found itself increasingly isolated from many of its neighbors.

The issue went far beyond President Nasser's personal leadership. As the largest Arab state, Egyptian influence in recent years has been a constant and natural factor in Arab politics; no plans for concerted Arab action could be made without Egyptian concurrence and participation. As the possessor of the area's largest armed force, the center of revolutionary change, and the most active Arab state in international affairs, the U.A.R. could not be shoved aside without generating a sharp reaction.

This reaction did not create the recent Arab-Israeli clash as a cynical maneuver to regain lost influence. As has been made clear, the elements of the crisis were all present in the situation and in the Arab suspicions of Israel's intent. But as the crisis developed, it seems clear that the U.A.R. saw in it an opportunity to reassert its "natural" leadership and this in connection with the one issue which most unites the Arabs. If a clash with Israel seemed imminent, the U.A.R. could not stand aloof from it or afford (with its large military force) to be halfhearted in its involvement. This does not mean that Egypt decided to launch an overt and aggressive attack on Israel at the head of united Arab armies. There is good reason to believe that President Nasser was pursuing a political rather than a military objective, and believed that a determined stand against what he and the Arabs felt to be the threat of Israeli action might force the United Nations to review the situation and institute a settlement more favorable to the Arabs. This was a return to the 1948 situation rather than to 1956; what was sought was not simply to curtail possible Israeli invasion, but to reopen the entire question of Palestine, including the refugees, in the hope that some new UN resolutions might result.

It is not yet possible accurately to assess the degree and form of Soviet responsibility for Arab actions. Apparently the Egyptians did not consult or clear with the Soviets when they closed the Gulf of Aqaba, and the Soviets did not support this action in their speeches at the Security Council. It has been claimed that Russian technicians participated in Syrian military action; if so, the number was small. There is no evidence that Russian personnel assisted the Egyptians.

It seems clear that the Soviets saw in the mounting tension between the Arabs and Israel an opportunity to increase their influence in the Arab world and to embarrass the

United States while its attention was absorbed in Vietnam. In general, Soviet objectives have been served by keeping the Arab-Israeli dispute simmering, but not allowing it to come to a boil. To settle the conflict would increase the stability of the area, which the Soviets do not want; to push it to overt conflict would imperil their large investment in some Arab lands and risk the danger of a global confrontation.

Here the Russians seem to have miscalculated as badly as the Arabs. They apparently assumed that the United States could and would control Israel on the brink of conflict, throwing the matter into the United Nations, where they could wage a prolonged diplomatic campaign in support of the Arabs. Part of their miscalculation seems to have been based on unrealistic estimates of Arab strength, which, if it could not defeat Israel (as any competent Soviet military analyst must have known), could at least stand off an attack until international intervention carried the matter from the battlefield to the debates of the United Nations.

Had UN intervention developed, the U.A.R. would have had a political triumph which would have restored its waning leadership, set forward the unity of the Arab world, and alleviated some of the deep frustrations which the Arab-Israeli impasse had created. This was one reason why President Nasser was willing to play the game of brinkmanship in the Gulf of Aqaba and on the southern borders of Israel, setting the stage for an Israeli response while continuing to believe that the worst would not happen.

But the worst did happen; the Arabs miscalculated their own military strength, the ability of the international community to intervene, and the determination of Israel to use direct military measures. The stunning defeat which followed has made that clear beyond all doubt; what it has not made clear is that any of the basic forces involved in the Arab reaction to Israel's presence has changed or been obliterated. That is the problem of the future, and any course of action which assumes that the recent war has settled the long-term issue will be unrealistic and unproductive.

IN THE WAKE OF WAR [2]

Throughout the nineteenth century no problem so persistently troubled European diplomacy as the Eastern Question, meaning the rivalry of the powers for dominance in the area from Cairo to Constantinople, where lay the strategic pathways between Europe and Asia. Then held in the decrepit and supposedly dying grip of the Ottoman Empire, the region was the focus of Russia's drive toward a warm-water outlet in the Mediterranean, Britain's need to control the road to India, France's dream of empire in the East, and at the end of the century, Germany's ambitions, spearheaded by the Berlin-to-Baghdad railway. The Question was which of the powers would succeed in becoming the favored protector of the Turk so as to gain the major influence in his dominions, keep rivals out, and be in the best position to inherit control when the Empire should break apart.

The process began, like so much else in modern history, with Napoleon, who, setting out at twenty-eight to recreate Alexander's empire from Egypt to the Indus, took Cairo in 1798, and though defeated by Nelson at the Battle of the Nile, went on by way of the Sinai Peninsula to invade Palestine. Here he laid siege to the port of Acre, whose fall he expected to open the way to Damascus and Constantinople, but he was stopped again by British naval guns and a landing force, which in support of the Turkish defense of the city frustrated the grand design. Even at the height of later triumphs he was heard to murmur, "I missed my destiny at St. Jean d'Acre."

The Eastern Question exploded anew in the ten-year crisis of 1830-1840 around the person of Mehemet Ali, ruler of Egypt as vassal of the Sultan, who rose in revolt with intent to make himself sovereign of an independent Muslim state covering Egypt, Arabia, and Syria (then including Pales-

[2] Article "In the Wake of War: Time and Reality in the Middle East," by Barbara W. Tuchman, historian, author of *The Guns of August, The Proud Tower*, and other books. *Atlantic*. 220:62-9. N. '67. Reprinted by permission of Russell & Volkening, Inc. and The Atlantic Monthly Company. Copyright © 1967 by The Atlantic Monthly Company, Boston, Mass.

tine). Russia seized this opportunity to come to the aid of the Sultan in the hope of gaining the Dardanelles, France adopted the cause of Mehemet, and Britain exerted desperate efforts, including another landing on the Syrian coast, to frustrate anyone other than a weak Turkey from bestriding the road to India.

The third stage was the Crimean War in 1855-1856. Precipitated by a quarrel over control of the Holy Places in Jerusalem, in reality the fight was an effort to contain Russia, conducted by Britain and France in support of Turkey. In 1860 in the Lebanon the struggle changed to an effort to contain France, led to the Levant by the imperial longings of Napoleon III in emulation of his uncle. The fourth stage followed in the 1870's when Britain acquired the Suez Canal and the Congress of Berlin was convened by the powers to limit Russia's gains after a successful war with Turkey. Once again Russia's old restless hunger for the south came into collision with Britain's path of Empire. "We shall have to choose," wrote the British Foreign Secretary, Lord Salisbury, before the Congress, "between allowing Russia to dominate over Syria and Mesopotamia or taking the country for ourselves." In the fifth stage Britain accomplished the preferred of these alternatives—in the modified form of Mandates—upon the fall of Turkey in 1918. At the present stage Britain has withdrawn, its place having been taken by the local inhabitants, Russia plays the same role as before, while the new superpower of the West operates by fits and starts, never quite positive what its world role should be.

Emerging Israel

Before World War I no one paid much attention to the political interests of the local inhabitants, which were, in fact, not exigent. When it came to holding sparsely inhabited Palestine as the fulcrum of the wobbling Ottoman Empire, it was an influx of Jews the Western powers thought of, rather than Arabs. The first version of the idea was Napoleon's. Having previously summoned the Arabs of Egypt to rise against their Turkish overlords, he issued a similar call on reaching Palestine to "all the Jews of Asia and Africa" to rally to his flag, restore the ancient Jerusalem, and "claim your political existence as a nation among nations." This was statehood before the Jews had thought of it. Under the circumstances of his expedition, Bonaparte's proclamation to the Jews was not very practical and had no consequences. The idea was later revived by Lord Palmerston, British Foreign Secretary during the Mehemet Ali affair, who urged the Sultan to encourage the return of the Jews to Palestine, where they could be a stabilizing factor against "any future evil designs of Mehemet Ali or his successor." This too was premature.

The Jews themselves at this time were either shut away in the ghettos of Central Europe or busy in the Western countries pursuing Emancipation, the child of that Enlightenment which was supposed to make man reasonable. Return to Palestine was not yet more than a traditional dream which had to await the coming of a Messiah. The country itself, which had once supported kingdoms and thoroughfares, temples and aqueducts, vineyards and fields of grain, had decayed during a thousand years of Arab habitation into a desolate tract, defoliated by goats. "There is not a mile of made road in the land from Dan to Beersheba," reported an officer of the Royal Engineers who conducted a survey for the Palestine Exploration Fund in 1878. Roads for wheeled transport, irrigation, drainage of malarial swamps, sanitation, seeding, and reforestation would all be required to revive the land.

These were the conditions which met the first trickle of Jewish colonists who began to come out of Russia under the goad of the nineteenth century's newly energized anti-Semitism. The early formulators of Zionism gave up waiting for a Messiah and asserted the doctrine of self-help. Rabbi Hirsch Kalischer of Prussia, author of *The Quest of Zion,* in 1860 had no great faith in the benevolence of the Western powers. He wanted Jewish soldiers to guard Jewish settlements and Jewish money raised from Jewish philanthropists to finance

the purchase of land, agricultural training, and loans to settlements until they could be self-supporting. In 1881 the
savage, state-instigated pogroms in Russia, followed by the
May Laws, prototype of Hitler's Nuremberg Laws, called
forth a famous pamphlet by Dr. Leo Pinsker of Odessa en-
titled *Auto-Emancipation,* of which the prefix is the part
that counts. The Jews must emancipate themselves, Pinsker
wrote, and reestablish themselves as a "living people." There
was no use complaining about anti-Semitism; it would go on
as long as the Jews were a ghost people without territory,
"ghosts of a dead nation walking among the living. There
is something unnatural about a people without territory just
as there is about a man without a shadow."

Impelled by the pogroms and the decitizenizing May
Laws, the exodus began, hesitantly, minutely, and without
benefit of intermediary power. On purchased land sold to
them as worthless by Turkish and Arab proprietors, the first
Jewish colonies, small, scattered, and feeble, gained a toe-
hold in the Jaffa area and in Galilee, where during the early
years they clung, always on the edge of ruin. Organized Zionism launched by Herzl came later at the turn of the century.

Whose Palestine?

The problem that no one, whether Zionists, Arab nationalists, or British, gave much thought to from the beginning was the Arab population of Palestine. Emir Hussein of
the Hejaz, sherif of Mecca, and his sons, Faisal and Abdullah,
who became kings of Iraq and Jordan respectively, were primarily concerned with Arabia and the region from Damascus
to Baghdad. Nor did the British during World War I regard
Arab nationalism as extending to Palestine, which always
had a special status in their dealings and was specifically "re-
served," both in the Sykes-Picot Treaty with France and in
the pledge negotiated with Hussein's family by the Arab
Bureau under Sir Henry McMahon in 1915. When Winston
Churchill as Colonial Secretary in 1922 lopped off Trans-
jordan from the rest of Palestine to create a new state by fiat,

he explicitly stated that "the whole of Palestine west of the Jordan" had been "excluded from Sir Henry McMahon's pledge."

The Jews' and Arabs' present titles to Palestine have been the subject of endless dispute. To state the matter as succinctly as possible, the modern history of these titles after the fall of the Turkish Empire is the following:

1. The Mandate conferred upon Britain by the principal Allied powers acting through the League of Nations, and ratified by them in 1922, gave international recognition to "the establishment in Palestine of a national home for the Jewish people" as promised by the Balfour Declaration, but did not grant territorial title or statehood to anybody. The Mandate had Class A status, which meant territory taken in charge without provision for future independence. The Arabs were nowhere mentioned by name but referred to as "other sections of the population" or "various peoples and communities" whose civil, religious, and personal rights were to be safeguarded.

2. Britain having relinquished the Mandate, the UN in 1947 voted for the partition of Palestine into a Jewish and an Arab state. The Jews accepted and obtained *de jure* recognition of their title in 1948. The Arabs rejected partition. In company with the armed forces of Egypt, Syria, Jordan, Lebanon, and Iraq, they attacked the Jews with the stated object of "forcible prevention" of a Jewish state, and were defeated. The Arab area allotted by the UN, somewhat reduced by the fortunes of war, was then annexed by Jordan (and in the Gaza area by Egypt) without ever having existed as a state. Consequently, no independent Arab state has existed in Palestine west of the Jordan since the Turkish conquest in 1072. How this leaves the question of title is a matter for international lawyers. Today, what is left of the area assigned to the Arabs under partition, now known as the West Bank and the Gaza Strip, is under the *de facto* control of Israel.

Perpetual Insult

As viewed by the Arabs this history has been one of perpetual insult. They are a frustrated and resentful people. In Napoleon's wake the return of Europeans to the Near East awoke them to the modern world and to the wine of nationalism. They found that during the long centuries of Islam's decline, the West had passed them by, and the infidel whom they considered inferior could now impose his will upon them. Unable to close the gap and resenting imperialism, they developed a sense of grievance which has outlasted their gain of independence in the twentieth century. Filtered through this grievance, history becomes a tale of the crimes committed against Arabs by others, beginning with the perfidy of the British in failing to keep a supposed promise to set up an independent Arab kingdom from the Red Sea to the Euphrates. Since the Arabs' own contribution to their liberation from the Turks was minimal (the Lawrence legend notwithstanding), they had no control over what happened thereafter and suffered the embitterment of dependence betrayed. Indeed, Arab history in the last fifty years would have been very different if they had played the determining role, with British help, in overthrow of the Turks instead of a token role in a British campaign.

It was only when Hussein's family, the Hashemites, had failed to unite Arab lands and peoples under their rule, when they had been pushed out of Syria and had lost Arabia to Ibn Saud, that the intrusion of the Jews, under the British promise of a "national home," appeared as the cause of Arab failure, a role it has played ever since.

Increasing Jewish immigration and settlement under the Mandate—bringing Western values and modern methods, planting orchards and fisheries and industries where there were none before, and making the land yield an income the Arab peasant never knew—proved an irritant which was worked up into a campaign of hostilities by the Mufti of Jerusalem, Haj Amin el-Husseini. A cousin of the Hashemites and a man of large ambitions, he hoped to rid Palestine of both Jews and British in order to set up a kingdom of his own. The riots and massacres and battles of the 1920's and 1930's, as the foundation of the enmity which has since swelled to trouble the world, were largely the work of that gleaming-eyed old man still alive today in Cairo.

To Wait Is to Win

Arab culture has its own values and manners and relationships of man to man and man to the land which were satisfactory to itself—or to the ruling class—as long as it remained separate unto itself. It was not the Jews but the modern world which brought its discontents. The Jewish presence in the Arab midst was the immediate visible symbol and a daily reminder of the difference in applied capacity. As an example of better living it threatened to upset the settled order of things. Originally it had been seen by such Arab partisans as T. E. Lawrence and by the Emir Faisal himself as an infusion of Western energy and skills acting in a partnership of Semitic cousins toward a renaissance of the Middle East. Instead it proved disruptive, as the impact of the West on a more primitive society has been known to be before.

In the huge expanse from the Nile to the Euphrates, Palestine, in Balfour's phrase, was a "small notch" and the Jews' right to a homeland there, in Weizmann's phrase, a matter of "relative equity," but to the Arabs, who keep trying to play a role equal to that of the Caliphate at its peak, the Jews serve as the reason for their nonsuccess.

The shock to the Arabs' ego when their combined forces failed to sweep the Jews into the sea in 1948 was profound. Their only defense was intransigence, a refusal to accept reality and an Eastern reliance on time: to wait is to win in the end. This explains their policy of attempting to isolate Israel by nonrecognition, boycott, blockade, severance of all contacts, and through intimidation, to prevent its contacts with other countries as well. Thus cut off, the Arabs believe,

Israel can never put down roots; its people will eventually pack up and go back where they came from, leaving the remnant to be easily destroyed. The favorite analogy is the Crusaders. Did the Arabs not wait two hundred years for those invaders to vanish? Why not again? The argument has bemused not only the Arabs but their Western partisans. It overlooks the essence: that Zionism is, after all, irredentism. Unlike the Crusaders, the Jews had been there before, which gives them a reason for staying. In their own minds they have come home.

For Nasser and other Arab leaders, it is impossible to admit the real lesson of the defeats of 1948, 1956, and 1967. It was unthinkable in 1948 that the Jews could have thrown back the attack by their own strength, hence the monster of World Zionism in explanation. The name, with its sinister "Z," conjures an image of diabolical power which the Arabs see as literally controlling the UN (hence partition) and all governments which have recognized Israel. Discrepancies, such as Russia's recognition, they meet with a bland, sincere gaze supposed to suffice the questioner. They may be bewildered but not embarrassed.

Anglo-French participation in the Suez campaign of 1956 was all they needed to prove the dependence of "Zionism" upon imperialism or vice versa, and the Anglo-French fiasco on the canal was enough to enable the Egyptians to overlook their military defeat by Israel in the desert and transform the whole campaign of 1956 into an Egyptian victory. There are victory monuments in Gaza and Cairo to prove it.

Last summer's crisis acquainted Westerners with the talent for fantasy that governs the Arab world—a world in which King Hussein and other leaders have found it worthwhile after the war to proclaim their people's readiness to "fight Israel to the last drop of blood," even though the recent opportunity to do just that was so conspicuously not embraced. Such talk may be only a liturgical ardor, which is the Arab habit of speech, but behind it the thinking is no less unreal. Hints of what they might be prepared to offer Israel in return for withdrawal, such as, by Jordan, unlimited access to the Wailing Wall, and by Egypt, free passage through the Strait of Tiran, are concessions which could be described as supererogatory.

What makes dealing with the Arabs even more uncertain is that they cannot be counted upon to act in their own best interest. The great common denominator of international dealings—a reasonable appreciation of self-interest—is lacking. This makes diplomacy in the Middle East something like playing poker against a beginner: it is impossible to say if a play represents concealed strength, calculated deception, mere vagary, or pure ignorance. Recently the Israeli commander at Qantara on the canal, explaining the difficulty of defense against the Egyptians' eccentric postwar shooting, said, "It isn't always easy to contemplate what they will do next. They are unique enemies really, because I don't think they know themselves."

Refuge in unreality is anyone's right, but the danger is to the rest of the world. The Arabs' refusal to accept the proof that they cannot destroy Israel militarily and their persistence in maintaining a state of war keep coals of belligerence burning at a focal point in the world's geography and sustain the belief that if only Israel were to vanish, their troubles would be over. In fact, their troubles are domestic and inter-Arab, and if Israel were to vanish tomorrow, the Arabs would be at each other's throats.

This kind of unreality is fostered in the whole mystique of the underdeveloped state and nowhere more than in the make-believe UN world of one-nation, one-vote. When nations are encouraged to ignore difference in capacity while they retain hostility, the result can be dangerous to everybody else. The hard reality of the matter is that the Arabs have committed themselves to an object—the elimination of Israel—which they are incapable of obtaining. They are incapable because, as was nakedly revealed last June, for all their ancient culture and modern jets, they belong, as far as the mass of their people is concerned, to the underdeveloped, or, to use the old-fashioned and franker word, backward, nations. This is the lesson of the war. Looking at the map, one asks how it was possible that the tiny sliver of Israel with a population the size of Connecticut's could defeat its enormous enemies, who were heavily armed in proportion to their overwhelming numbers and could attack from three sides. The improbable verdict was no accident. In the floods of discussion since then, the clash of arms is almost forgotten, but the war *was* in fact the real test, and the Israeli victory no magician's trick, as it has come to seem to the Arabs and their partisans. It was valid—for the valid reason of superior ability.

The Arabs had the power, but they could not deliver. Nothing else to be seen on the battlefields was so significant as a series of huge tanks, whose *raison d'être* is mobility, which are designed to carry war to the enemy, dug into sandpits by the Egyptians for use as field artillery. This was from no shortage of equipment, nor from ineptness or ignorance. It could only mean, as the unreadiness of their air forces likewise suggests, that under conditions of modern warfare against a modern enemy however small, the Arabs have no stomach for the attack which figures so conspicuously in their speeches. If they did not have it in June, they are not likely to acquire it, for it is doubtful, in my opinion, that they will ever be, relatively, in a better position to accomplish their object than they were in the last crisis.

When history happens under one's eyes one should learn something. To me it suggests that the underdeveloped nations are not closing the gap; on the contrary, the gap is widening. They cannot catch up in social progress, education, and food with their exploding populations. With the present technology of weapons, nuclear or not, numbers, even vast superiority of numbers, are not and will not be determining. Nor will possession of modern weapons without the skill and self-confidence to operate them.

The Arabs' belief that if only they wait long enough they will overcome seems to many unanswerable. Yet population, if it outstrips food, can lead to weakness rather than strength, as in the case of India. On the other hand, Israel may, in the long run, share in the predicted decline of the West. Conversely, the degree of challenge Israel must meet merely to survive may exempt it from that fate. None of these considerations are absolute, and they raise the crucial question: time is on whose side in the Middle East?

Israel's Problems Today

Israel's difficulties, both short-range and long-range, are extreme. Governing occupied territory with an undetermined political future leaves unlimited openings for trouble. Many inhabitants are afraid to cooperate for fear of reprisal if the regime should change; others conspire for change. Resettling the refugees or restoring a viable economy in areas whose normal markets are cut off is no easier, especially at a time when Israel's own economy is depressed. Its economy suffers from retrenchment, the rigid grip of labor bureaucracy on employment practices, and the continuing need for foreign investment.

The refugees have become a stone of Sisyphus. Israel has taken 500,000 Oriental Jews from the Arab states, some recruited, some expelled, because their absorption was in Israel's interest. The Arab refugees on the other hand were useful to the Arab states only if *not* absorbed, but kept in camps as living propaganda and as a source of guerrillas and infiltrators. Although the oil-producing Arab states count their daily income in millions, Arab unity has not extended to philanthropy, and the refugees for the last nineteen years have been left a charge on the international community, with 70 per cent of the funds provided by the United States.

In the camps of Gaza and the West Bank they are still in their native land—that is, within the confines of Palestine, although they have lost their native homes and villages. Unhappy enough at best, this condition has been made to seem, under the whip of the Palestine Liberation Organization's [PLO] propaganda, permanently unacceptable. A young man in a refugee camp at Jenin on the West Bank, of sufficient ambition to have obtained an education and a position as chemistry teacher in a vocational school, explained that his native village was seven kilometers away, inside Israel, in the same valley of Jezreel as Jenin. Yet for him it was unthinkable to leave the camp and settle "here"; nothing else but back "there" on his native ground would do.

"They have taken our homes and must be made to give them back" is the single, insistent, recurring theme of the Palestinian Arabs. Their true misfortune is that they are encouraged by Cairo and Damascus and PLO agitators to believe the aim is realizable.

The refugees became refugees when they left their homes in 1948 under the impact of the war launched, and lost, by their compatriots. Israel in the years since 1948 refused to readmit them chiefly because, while its neighbors maintained a state of war, Israel could not afford a potential fifth column of half a million people in a state of two and a half million. Now victory has laid the problem in Israel's lap, with long-range implications profoundly disturbing to the state.

They come down to this: can Israel remain a Jewish state? It is caught in a central dilemma: to enlarge its boundaries for the sake of defensible frontiers means absorbing over a million Arabs who, outbreeding the Jews, could become a majority. To withdraw to prewar boundaries would be to keep a Jewish majority but return to the insecurity of a position that can only be defended by taking the offensive.

With Arabs of Israeli citizenship already amounting to 11 per cent of the population, and Oriental Jews numbering 29 per cent, the fear of becoming orientalized already exists. In the early years of the national home some Jews, notably the distinguished first president of the Hebrew University, Dr. Judah Magnes, foresaw or believed in the necessity of a binational state. The subject of profound schism then, his ideas were rejected. Although in the new context since the war they may be revived, few Israelis today would be ready to argue openly that their country could or should give up its character as a Jewish state.

From their point of view the only desirable solution of the dilemma is the Arabs' formal abandonment of belligerency, which would permit Israel to live more or less safely without having to extend its territory to take in an unwanted Arab population. This is Israel's main objective—establishment of orderly relations between neighboring states—open borders, trade, commerce, contact, transit, the normal fabric of a legal peace. That is why Israel is so insistent on direct negotiation. The good offices of an intermediary, which would relieve the Arabs of the necessity of meeting the Israelis face to face and of accepting Israel's existence by peace treaty, would be no improvement over the past.

The Arabs' Impasse

Nations are not usually content to win wars for nothing, and in that respect there is no reason why this war should be different from all others. The victors in World Wars I and II took reparations and territory, redrew boundaries, and imposed armies of occupation (still in force) to preserve security. Should Israel do less? It has retaken Jerusalem in the spirit that France retook Alsace. As regards the rest, Israel is unlikely, unless forced, to withdraw quietly to its prewar situation with no *quid pro quo* in national security.

This will not soon be forthcoming. Except for the Palestinians of the West Bank, who have begun to grope toward a solution, the Arab states at the time of writing show no visible signs of coming to any terms even remotely related to the verdict of the war. They are still searching for some magic that will cancel the result of those six days last June. Until they discover that no magic, or pretense of moderation, or others' mediation, or Russian maneuvers, or even by

Tito's running interference, will turn back the clock, they will not recognize Israel, which is the one gain it must have.

Possibly if Nasser falls, a new leader could effect a change of opinion. The Arabs as a people are highly emotional and easily swayed. They "could be swung on an idea as on a cord," wrote T. E. Lawrence. With little sense of participation in government, the average Arab likes to be told what to think by an admired leader. Public opinion is volatile, and the story is told of a prominent Egyptian editor to whom it was suggested that his anti-American tirades were creating an unfortunate climate of opinion just at a period of negotiations for foreign aid. "Don't worry, my dear fellow, I can change that in three days," the editor said. Asked if he could do the same with regard to Israel, he thought for a moment and replied, "That would take ten."

Short of such a revolution, it is false to pretend that the impasse rests on an undying injustice to the refugees which only recovery of their native homes can resolve. On that basis we should give America back to the Indians, or at the very least, Texas back to the Mexicans, or perhaps Hawaii back to whatever Hawaiians have survived our intrusion into their land. History is full of the displacement of peoples; it closes over them and moves on, massively indifferent. That may not be justice, but it is nature. Perfect justice rarely regulates the affairs of nations, and we are doing well if we can achieve "relative equity," which is not hard to locate as between Jews with less than one per cent of the 1.2 million square miles liberated from the Turks, and the Arabs with all the rest.

The refugees in any case are better off than most uprooted peoples since they are still in their native land, where they could settle, if politics allowed, into the same economy, agriculture, customs, language as before. The undercultivated West Bank has room for—and with introduction of modern methods, could support—them all, including the majority from the overcrowded Gaza Strip. With Israeli know-how in resettlement, with the waiting land and peoples, with perhaps nuclear power for irrigation by desalinization, and with UN (meaning U.S.) financing, here at least is an opportunity for constructive action. It has been done before, in 1924 when 500,000 Greek refugees from Turkey were re-settled in Greece by an American High Commissioner under League of Nations auspices. Is capacity less today? The cost, according to estimates, might be a billion dollars—equal to the cost of running the war in Vietnam for two weeks.

Meanwhile the Arabs wait with amputated territories, Israel waits with dangerous burdens, and the question again is: whose side does time serve? The Arabs will say they don't care how long they wait, which is another way of escaping the present. Meanwhile they have lost tremendous leverage—in the headwaters of the Jordan, the Syrian pipeline, the Suez Canal, the Sinai oil wells, and the Strait of Tiran, all now under Israel's control.

How long Israel can hold the occupied territories without coming to some announced decision is an open question. The longer the present situation lasts, with the investment of effort in paving roads, opening schools, extending utilities and sanitation, the harder it will be to turn back the West Bank, which is the major problem. If the Arabs will not make peace, the stern irony of conquest may bring Israel territory it does not need from a war it did not want, and ultimately cost its integrity as a Jewish state.

Wanted: New Immigrants

Under this cloud the mood in Israel since the war is sober and worried. Some realize with sadness that things can never be the same as before; others believe it is time to learn to think in terms of power. The older generation, more ded-icated to the founding Zionist tradition, sees no reason why Israel, given normalcy of relations, cannot function forever at its pre-June territorial size as a kind of Switzerland of the Middle East. But to fill up the Negev and ground the state firmly and preserve its Jewish identity, they insist Israel must have increased Jewish immigration from the free world. They want a population of 5 million by the end of the century. Aliya, or immigration (literally "ascent") , is the theme of speeches, conferences, exhortations every other day, with Prime Minister Eshkol, like Ben-Gurion before him, its most persistent and fervent exponent. To the preachers of Aliya this is the most urgent matter of all, and the cutting off of 3 million Jews in Russia is a greater tragedy than Arab hostility. They have convinced themselves that an inflow of 30,000 to 40,000 a year from the United States, Latin America, and other countries of the West is feasible, and with natural increase they should attain the 5 million goal and secure the Jewish character of the state.

To what degree they are self-deceived, or deceived by the Zionist organizations abroad, who must believe in emigration in order to stay in business, is a matter of opinion. What is history, however, is that the three Aliyas which went into the making of the state—from Russia, from Hitler's Europe, and from the Arab countries—all came because they were pushed, because conditions in those countries were made intolerable. That people will leave a more comfortable for a less comfortable society minus a propellant is not the normal way of things. Officially the Israelis count on idealism, but they do not put a propellant beyond the bounds of possibility.

Whatever the solution, the Jews of Palestine have reached a third stage in their development: from dependence to independence to power. Of necessity thoughtful citizens are reexamining their country's purpose and future. What is to be its role in the Middle East and its reason for existence? It is not, said Simon Peres, former Deputy Minister of Defense and one of the country's most influential political figures, to be "just another little America." But what it is to be, few in the present state of flux could say with certainty. Half a century ago Sir Mark Sykes suggested that it might be the destiny of the Jews "to be the bridge between Asia and

Europe, to bring the spirituality of Asia to Europe and the vitality of Europe to Asia." Sykes was a fervent advocate both of a revived Arab nation and of the Zionist return, and it is one of history's tragedies that his position, which seemed natural then, should seem unnatural now.

The Cold War

What of the powers and the Eastern Question today? Russia's interest, as before, is a "sphere of influence," and though ideology may have changed, the method, as before, is to establish a client relationship; with the Turkish Empire then, with its successor states today—at least those which are politically susceptible. Russia's aim is to extend the list by political action in the oil-rich domains, where American influence so far predominates.

As an American diplomat has put it, there are three wars in the Middle East: Arab-Israeli, Arab-Arab, and the cold war. Russia cannot let slip its position as the Arabs' major friend. China is in the background, and the cold war is no longer really or only a Communist-capitalist war, but slowly transforming itself, with gaps, into an Afro-Arab-Asian front against the white West. Where that leaves Russia, only history will tell. It is interesting that a recent Black Power statement, though largely lunatic, unhesitatingly placed the Soviet Union among the "whites," and an Israeli tape, made during the war when the Syrian troops broke, recorded a Russian voice crying, "The blacks are running!"

Vis-à-vis Israel, Russia doubtless accepts its existence as a permanent reality while from time to time, to keep them happy, encouraging the Arabs in the belief that they can someday eliminate it. Israel is useful to Russia as a goad of Arab fears and antagonisms. A settled peace is not necessarily a Soviet interest in the Middle East, nor war either, but rather what the *Economist* has called "a little exploitable unrest."

Since the interest of the United States, on the other hand, is a stable peace, its problem is that much more difficult. It must deal as equably as possible with both Israel and the Arabs, including the radical Arab states, however perverse their behavior. The Arabs, with their sense of injury, their unreality, their extremism, large territory, and great numbers, are a fact of life. They are there. The Israelis, on the other hand, have vocal friends, but their difficulty is that they have no leverage; they *have* to be on our side, they do not have to be wooed. Status as a threat or nuisance sufficient to require being appeased is an asset in international affairs which they lack.

In view of pressures by devoted partisans of either side, American policy is not simple either to formulate or apply. Aramco [Arabian American Oil Company] is the largest single American investment abroad, and oil makes larger profits than any other business in the world besides having a very large number of stockholders. The great fear of the oil companies is of nationalization, which would certainly be a consequence if the Arab monarchies should give way to pro-Soviet regimes.

In the long run the swell of decolonization will propel the oil companies out of the Middle East, but businessmen, being preoccupied with the present, are not historians. The oil men have had comfortable arrangements with the sheikhs and sovereigns for a long time which they do not like to see disturbed, and they deplore all this turmoil, engendered, as they see it, by the intrusion of Israel. Bent on keeping the feudal rulers in power, they want the United States to give the Saudis, Kuwaitis, and others a handle against the radicals by forcing Israel to withdraw, thus proving American friendship and usefulness—and an alternative to Russia. An effort of that kind, if successful, would only convince the radical Arab states that intransigence pays off, which would hardly improve the situation. From the American point of view, if something positive is to be gained from the late crisis, it can only be in some form of Arab acceptance of Israel as a fact of life. How far Washington is prepared to work for this or the oil lobby to sanction it is another matter.

The Global Treadmill

The problems of a superpower are heavy. No matter what turns up, no matter where on the globe, American power is engaged in it as if the United States were caught on a global treadmill from which it cannot step down. The larger our establishment, with connections in every corner of every continent, periscopes in the seven seas, and aerial reconnaissance daily circling the globe, the more we respond to every quiver and feel obliged to influence every event so that it does not go against us. The penalty of gigantism is to think in too large terms, and we operate in terms of Them and Us as if that dichotomy determined all destinies. We are too little aware of variations, individualities, ancient histories, local character, and local pressures, which are the real determinants on the spot. No Pax Americana can accommodate or encompass them. We cannot make others go our way by aid or by arms or by advice which starts out with a few advisers and ends up as major war.

The connection between the Middle East and Vietnam is the evidence that gigantism is ineffective. Russia could not control developments for its clients, nor could all its vast armaments and all the Arab states defeat one small but determined country. The American hand in the Middle East crisis before hostilities was likewise unavailing. Washington's attempt, allowing two weeks to organize a regatta for the Gulf of Aqaba, was unrealistic even if based on an Israeli assurance of a two-week leeway. No such assurance given in Washington could control a crisis situation. With both sides "eyeball to eyeball," as were the powers in 1914, and fully mobilized at huge cost upon their already weakened economies, and with tension building up unbearably, the assumption that the dangers would wait and emotions obediently subdue themselves while Washington pursued consensus was an example of the superpower ignoring local realities. If the result proved fortunate for Israel in the end, in that Israel broke an impossible situation by unaided effort, that was not because of any policy the United States had ready.

In Vietnam, with all our weaponry, modern skills, and physical presence, America can do no better than Russia in the Middle East. We are precluded from using total military power because victory won by that means would defeat its purpose. Anything less, though it be the greatest expenditure of men, arms, and money since World War II, evidently cannot achieve what we want. In a world which contains and must continue to contain other cultures, other values, other determinations, superpower, it would appear, has its limits—which is just as well. A world with a single set of values is neither possible nor desirable—nor necessary for security. We could well afford to get off the global treadmill from time to time, for if superpower cannot give us confidence in our own society, and the strength to put it in shape, it can do nothing.

III. THE WAR AND ITS AFTERMATH

EDITOR'S INTRODUCTION

Not the least astonishing aspect of the Arab-Israeli war was its brevity. As the British military historian B. H. Liddell Hart points out in the first article in this section, the six-day war demonstrated to both East and West that the Israeli armed forces possessed surprising capability in routing the heavily-equipped and numerous Arab forces. The impact of these days on Israel is presented in the next article, "Letter from Israel," taken from the *New Yorker*. In view of the re-sounding defeat, Nasser's first response, to declare that American and British aircraft had aided the Israelis, might have been expected. Reporting from Cairo, the journalist Trevor Armbrister explains, in the third selection, that "Nasser had to break diplomatic relations [with the United States] to give credence to his claim of Western intervention." The collapse of the Arab armies also engendered Russian disgust since Moscow had been the chief supplier of Egyptian arms.

In the immediate aftermath of the war, many observers saw mirrored in the Arab defeat a setback to Soviet influence in the Middle East. This illusion was soon dispelled when it was seen that the very failure of the Arabs to impose their military might on Israel put them into ever greater bondage to the Soviets. In agreeing to reequip the Arabs, the Russians would no doubt expect something in return, such as Soviet bases on the Mediterranean. Meanwhile, the Arabs have mounted a continuing and surprisingly strong guerrilla offensive. In a report from the Middle East, New York *Times* correspondent Drew Middleton makes it clear that the guer-rillas will receive support from the Arab leaders, even if the guerrilla movement proves a danger to the ruling class itself.

Both Moscow and Washington were anxious about avoiding an open clash. In this respect, the dangerous games the great powers are tempted to play in the Middle East are carried on in keeping with the openly expressed desire to avoid direct involvement of either Russian or American forces. The West would like to see Israel and the Arabs come to terms with each other as soon as possible, and even Moscow makes gestures in the direction of stability. But neither East nor West finds it easy to reconcile Arab pride with Israeli demands that the Arabs recognize the existence of a separate Jewish state in the Middle East. While it is impossible to predict the outcome from the negotiating positions maintained by both victors and vanquished, there seems a dubious chance, as Amnon Rubinstein of Hebrew University puts it, of Israel's finding peace through military victory.

STRATEGY OF A WAR [1]

The most crucial stroke in the Six-Day War of 1967 was the first, the air stroke—or, in modern parlance, the "air strike." The details were revealed very soon after the event, presumably with the permission of the Israeli censorship which in 1956 had been extremely, and in some respects absurdly, secretive. In particular, a valid chapter in the account of war by Randolph and Winston Churchill, brought out as a paperback only two months after it ended, provided a remarkably clear picture of the techniques developed by General Weizmann, the creator of the Israel air force, and applied by General Hod, its present chief, who, personally, played an even more decisive role in the first fateful hours of 5 June than is yet known outside a small circle.

Besides the combined calculation and subtlety of a plan that paralyzed the whole of the numerically superior Egyptian air force at the outset, the staggering ground turn-around time of the Israelis, barely seven and a half minutes, was it-

[1] From article by B. H. Liddell Hart, author of works on military theory and strategy. *Encounter* (London). 30:16-20. F. '68. Reprinted by permission.

self a great contribution to surprise—enabling many of the Israeli pilots to start on a second sortie within an hour, and make eight sorties in the day, compared with the Egyptian reckoning that they might manage to do two. It is no wonder that Nasser sought to disguise his *débâcle* by asserting that American and British aircraft had reinforced Israel's.

Numerous reports have emphasized the effect of the way that Israeli air attack came in from unexpected directions, and how upsetting that proved....

Blitzkrieg

The whole course of the Israeli campaign, a perfect *Blitzkrieg,* was of particular interest to me because it was the best demonstration yet of the theory of the strategy of indirect approach, and in its subtler sense of seeking and exploiting "the line of least expectation"—a theory evolved nearly forty years ago. The Germans, to my chagrin, applied it in 1940, under Guderian's inspiration and influence. But even Guderian or Rommel, generous as they were in acknowledgment, did not grasp the subtler side of it so well as the Israeli leaders have done since 1948: the first of three successive tests they have had to meet, when Yadin (now more famous as an archeologist through his discoveries at Masada) was the directing brain of their strategy, and Allon (now minister of labor and a potential prime minister) commanded in turn the offensives in Upper Galilee, in the center at Lydda, and then on the southern front against the Egyptians. With each test, the Israelis have improved—contradicting the experience of history that armies learn only from defeat not victory.

What struck me most in their latest campaign, compared with the second in 1956, was the significant development of the Israeli plan and operations in combining the strategical offensive with the tactical defensive—in getting round the back of the Egyptians in Sinai after the opening penetrations and, by blocking their lines of retreat, forcing them to attack in trying to escape.

It was also significant that the center "division" under General Yoffe, which established the main blocking position, at the Mitla Pass, gained its initial penetration of the frontier line by taking a route through sand-dunes that the Egyptians evidently believed to be impassable. It came as more of a surprise to the Egyptians because this route, by a rough desert track some twenty miles south of Rafa and El Arish, between the coastal and Ismailia roads, had not been used or attempted in 1956. It was found that only a mere company, with a few antitank guns, was covering this route—and was soon overrun. That was fortunate, as the main armored force on the coastal route, under General Tal, met much tougher resistance than in 1956—until Yoffe's armored force brought its flank, and rear-menacing, leverage to bear.

Tal's force started by tackling two opposing divisions on the north coast, in the Gaza Strip and the El Arish area. That meant forcing successively two fortified positions, the first of them some eight miles deep. But he levered away the resistance by inner flanking moves, while seeking to lure the Egyptian armor into counterattacking his forces, which kept well-balanced and ready to shatter counterattacks. The bait failed, as the Egyptians stuck to the defensive, but their very passivity helped Tal's forces to surround and destroy them piecemeal, particularly when they eventually began to fall back towards the Suez Canal under the threat to their flank and rear. Sweeping forward past Romani, Tal's right prong reached the canal at Qantara and Ismailia on the fourth morning.

After a hard fight at El Arish, eventually captured by a night attack with mechanized infantry, he had divided his "division," sending a powerful left prong southwestward into the desert interior to combine with Yoffe's force, and block another of the Egyptians' escape routes at Bir Gafgafa. There it met a fresh armored brigade (equipped with the latest Russian T.55 tanks) that had been sent forward from the Suez Canal to keep open this bottleneck. But this was kept in check for over two hours by an Israeli regiment of light tanks, despite heavy casualties, until a reinforcement of more powerful tanks (Pattons and Centurions armed with the 105mm. gun) came up to reinforce it, and liquidate the Egyptian armored brigade.

Yoffe's "division" was equipped with modernized Centurion tanks armed with the 105mm. gun, and he reported that these proved more effective than the T.54 (and even the latest T.55 Russian tank) used by the Egyptians. His initial advance met no serious opposition owing to taking an unexpected route through the sand dunes. But in the fighting on the second day he had heavier losses when linking up with Tal's "division" in the battle for El Arish. By the time his leading battalion reached the road junction of Heitan, on its way to Mitla Pass, it had only fourteen tanks left, and of these seven were towing the other seven, which were out of fuel. But they sufficed to create a blocking position, which was cemented on the third morning when Yoffe got up reinforcements to his advanced battalion, as well as some more petrol to restore its full mobility. After spending the day in rounding up thousands of prisoners from the blocked Egyptian forces, whose vehicles were caught and destroyed by the Israeli air force, Yoffe resumed his advance to the Suez Canal on the fourth morning, and arrived on the canal in the afternoon at Port Taufiq, opposite Suez.

Sharon's "division" on the left wing was also deployed and employed in a dual-pronged way, and with the deceptive use of dummy tanks conveyed the impression that it was aiming at a dash through Quntilla to the Gulf of Aqaba and the capture of Sharm el Sheikh, as in 1956, whereas it was actually thrusting westward to Suez.

In its initial drive southwestward Sharon's "division" obliquely crossed the route taken by Yoffe's, and thus came down on the flank of a strong Egyptian tank and infantry force that was holding Abu Agheila, where it had a very tough fight, and then on the rear of the Egyptian armored force that was poised near Themed for an advance to capture Elath, Israel's port at the top of the Gulf of Aqaba. Although it did not achieve as spectacular a bag of prisoners as the other two "divisions" did, its distracting effect made an invaluable contribution to the success, and rapidity, of their westward drive to the Suez Canal.

The three Israeli "divisions" on the Sinai front, which had to face seven Egyptian divisions, were under the control of General Gavish, who was in charge of the Southern Command.

In sum, the plan was a superb application of the strategy of indirect approach, and its corollary of choosing "the line of least expectation," to throw the opponent off balance.

On the Jordanian front, rugged and more constricted, there was less scope for maneuver, and the handicaps on it were greater because of the Israelis' very natural, and passionate, desire to occupy the whole city of Jerusalem as soon as possible. Moreover they had not expected that King Hussein would actually take the offensive in aid of Nasser, in view of the way that Nasser has sowed dissension in Jordan.

Israeli Expectations

When visiting Israel in 1960 as a guest, I had lengthy discussions, some on the map, with Generals Laskov, then chief of staff, and Rabin, then vice chief, about their course of action in any future war. From these discussions it was evident that the contingency with which they were most concerned was that Hussein might be overthrown by a Nasserite plot and—in that case they would advance into Jordan immediately before Egyptian and other Arab forces could move in and threaten to cut off their own semi-isolated position in Jerusalem, and worse still, cut through Israel's narrow waist, which north of Tel Aviv is barely ten miles wide—so that an armored force, striking by surprise from the Jordan frontier, might reach the coast in half an hour. But so long as Hussein remained on his throne, and in power, the Israelis were in general content to preserve a defensive posture and avoid any provocation to Jordan that might push it into the embrace of Nasser.

The cramping conditions around Jerusalem, and the unexpectedness of King Hussein's active intervention in the war, hindered any such wide and subtle maneuvering as that carried on on the southern front in Sinai. Moreover, when this Jordanian offensive intervention became clear, the Israelis' intense emotional urge to seize the opportunity of regaining possession of Jerusalem as a whole was a handicap on any subtle strategy by General Narkis, the commander of the Central Command. Even so, the operation was carried out by a series of local flanking moves with an armored brigade, a dismounted paratroop brigade, and an infantry brigade—and despite stiff resistance from the Jordanian troops the Israelis achieved their prime objective by nightfall on the third day, while exploiting their success by the speedy capture of Jericho on the West Bank of the Jordan and Hebron, south of Jerusalem. A loss of some 200 killed was not a high price for such a victory, in which the Jordanian casualties were estimated at about 8,000.

Meanwhile the four brigades of the Northern Command, under General Elazar, overran the northern part of Jordania west of the river, by pincer moves against Jenin and Nablus, each of an indirect kind and culminating in a rear attack. Their swift success was greatly helped by the way they unbalanced their opponent's dispositions, as well as by the Air Force's help in disrupting the opponent's efforts to regroup his forces.

In the next, and final stage, of the war—starting on 9 June, the fifth day—the Israelis switched their northern effort against the Syrian forces, whose artillery had been battering the Israeli settlements around and north of Lake Tiberias, the Sea of Galilee, since the outbreak of war—from the high ground east of the valley. Time was short because of the "cease-fire" for which the United Nations assembly was calling, so that here again the time factor was a handicap on effective use of the indirect approach and maneuver. Thus the Israeli moves were narrower and more direct than they need otherwise have been—and their losses consequently heavier. Nevertheless, they succeeded in clearing the heights by the second evening—with a total loss of little more than four hundred (which was far less than the Syrians suffered)—and could easily have driven on into Damascus, the Syrian capital, by the third day but for the "cease-fire."

If they had driven on eastward far enough to reach the area inhabited by the Druses [a people and religious sect living in the Lebanon Mountains of Syria], they might have helped to establish an independent state there that could have been a buffer between Syria and Jordan—to the benefit of the latter, and of the future of the Middle East. . . .

As to the postwar situation and the question of a peace settlement, the experience of the past twenty years—and indeed, the last half century's history of the Middle East—shows all too clearly that little can be expected from negotiations, but only from time and stability. Any settlement is likely to take a long time, and it is foolish for the Western powers to indulge in hopes of hastening the process—either from altruism or short-sighted concern for their own short-term interests.

Meanwhile in the present political turbulence, it is most important for Israel's security that she should remain in control of the whole, or almost the whole, of the area she has conquered—Sinai, the part of Jordan west of the River Jordan, and the high ground in Syria from which the Syrians have been able to harass the Huleh Valley and Galilee. For security of defense, it might possibly suffice if Israel retains the high ground from Jerusalem to Jenin, exclusive of Nablus, and this would avoid the disadvantage of taking in a large number of Arabs, but it would mean a somewhat longer frontier, and one more difficult to guard against guerrilla infiltration. In Sinai, no such problem arises, as the Arab population is small, but it might suffice strategically, and be less cause of friction, if the Israeli frontier ran along the heights north and south of the Mitla Pass.

It is to be hoped that the Israelis will be able to withstand any pressure to give up this "security area," and that there will be no British or American pressure, even well-meaning pressure, to give it up in the supposed hope of conciliating her enemies. Past experience of Arab politicians offers no ground of hope in such conciliation. A better chance lies in the possibility of nonpolitical Arabs coming to see the advantages of cooperation with Israel for the benefit of the Middle East in general.

I also think that Israel should not only be accorded freedom of passage through the Suez Canal, but that the canal itself should be internationalized. The Israelis might well, and wisely, decide to stay there until it is made, and accepted as, a truly international waterway.

LETTER FROM ISRAEL [2]

Thursday, June 1st [1967]: An American Jew of German descent who now makes his home in New York arrived at Lod Airport, in Tel Aviv, and got into a battered old taxi, which was already carrying a few passengers, for the ride to Jerusalem. His daughter was spending her junior year abroad at the Hebrew University, and he was going to try to persuade her to come home. He thought he recognized a pattern to events, and he was afraid. He had been merely depressed by previous violations of international guarantees to Israel—free passage through the Suez Canal, for example, or free access to the Old City of Jerusalem—but the blockade of the Strait of Tiran had made it impossible for him to sleep. While the great powers temporized and rationalized, he felt that a little country's territory and morale were being worn away. It reminded him exactly, he said, of the dismemberment of

[2] From article by Renata Adler, correspondent. *New Yorker.* 43:114+. Je. 17, '67. Excerpts from the article "Letter from Israel" by Renata Adler, reprinted by permission; © 1967 The New Yorker Magazine, Inc.

Czechoslovakia. Foreseeing, as he thought, its inevitable consequences, he wanted his daughter home. The taxi picked up several passengers along the road (which was nearly deserted but still lined with the carapaces of armored cars destroyed in 1948), and on the outskirts of Jerusalem the worried gentleman got out.

The city itself resembled, on that Thursday before the war, a sunny, sparsely populated colony for the infirm. Even the taxi driver wore a leather glove concealing an artificial hand, and most of the pedestrians (there were few cars) were either old or lame or very young and scruffy and truant-looking. The King David Hotel was nearly empty, except for some journalists and a few indomitable tourists. Avram Zvi, the large, middle-aged manager of the King David, engaged his guests in merry conversation, and new arrivals at the reception desk were offered rooms overlooking the Old City ("There you have the view") or overlooking the YMCA on the Israeli side ("There it is more safe"). The entrance to the YMCA—the scene of bitter fighting in 1948—was concealed by sandbags, but aside from these, and from the strange emptiness of the streets, Jerusalem had made no obvious preparations for a state of war. From some windows, the sound of radios tuned to Kol Yisroel, the Voice of Israel, drifted over the city. Since the early stages of mobilization, Kol Yisroel had been broadcasting only Israeli songs, Hebrew news, and (recognizing that few Israelis over twenty-five speak the national language perfectly) two news programs each day in French, Rumanian, Yiddish, English, Hungarian, Russian, and Ladino. On Thursday, June 1st, Kol Yisroel announced in eight languages that the Mapai Party of Premier Levi Eshkol had at last formed an emergency cabinet with the Gahal Party and with Ben-Gurion's Rafi Party (although BiGi himself, as the Israelis call him, had remained aloof), and that the Rafi Party's General Moshe Dayan had been appointed minister of defense.

Friday, June 2nd, in Tel Aviv was listless and stiflingly dull. The city was uncrowded, but it seemed as though everyone might merely be taking a siesta. In fact, quite a number of people were off at the beaches and swimming pools. Several international journalists, having exhausted their color stories about a proud, encircled people unafraid in the face of overwhelming odds, or the economic impossibility of maintaining a civilian army on perpetual alert, were preparing to go home. It began to seem that even the appointment of Dayan had been only a bit of stage business in the little off-Hot Line theatrical production to which the small nations seemed now to be reduced. It appeared that Nasser's production had all the angels, and that even *lack* of initiative had passed out of the hands of Israel to London, Paris, and Washington. The oppressive sense that nothing at all was going to happen created the feeling that access to the world's attention was being closed along with passage through the Gulf of Aqaba. Israel seemed about to drop out of the news.

At the Chaim Weizmann Institute, in Rehovoth, on Friday night, however, people seemed both more active and less sanguine than in Tel Aviv. The Orthodox rabbis in Jerusalem had announced that for the Army the obligations of the Sabbath were temporarily suspended, and some of the inhabitants of Rehovoth felt that war might begin the following morning. (The rabbis had earlier suspended their campaign against autopsies, and this sort of concession had led some people to expect war on every Sabbath since the beginning of the crisis.) The Weizmann Institute—whose cornerstone was laid to the sound of distant gunfire in 1946—has become over the years a kind of dream haven for pure science, an intellectual aerie amid green lawns, orange groves, and bougainvillaea between Jerusalem and Tel Aviv. Agricultural research at the Institute had contributed vitally to Israel's unprecedented programs for reclamation of the soil. Theoretical research in nuclear physics and chemistry had succeeded so well that scientists were turning their attention to newer fields, like high-energy physics and research with RNA [ribonucleic acid]. One of the country's crowning and yet most characteristic achievements, the Institute had for weeks been on an emergency footing. (For one thing, a prevailing myth among the Arab nations that an atomic bomb was housed there made it a prime target for enemy bombing.) Of forty-three men at work on constructing a new building for the Institute, forty had been called up into the army. Those members of the scientific staff who had not been called up as soldiers or military advisers, or put to work on special scientific projects related to mobilization, were busy taping windows or wrapping up sensitive or explosive instruments against the threat of attack. The children of the community were taking first-aid courses. Research biologists who had taken medical degrees but never actually treated patients were setting up emergency clinics. Sandbags and supports for basement ceilings were being put up in all the buildings of the Institute. In addition to their other work, scientists with walkie-talkies strapped to their waists took part in patrolling the Institute's grounds at night.

Waiting for War

War, of course, did not break out on Saturday morning. Instead, wives and children took advantage of the Sabbath to join their men for picnics at the front. In effect, the front in a country of Israel's size was everywhere. But border *kibbutzim* [cooperative farms, collectively armed, operated on a commercial basis] like Nir Yitzhak and Shalom Karem, at the edge of the Negev and the Gaza Strip, were particularly full of families reclining with picnic baskets under the trees near the webby, shapeless tents in which the soldiers had been living for two weeks. The station wagons parked by the side of the road, and the tanned, rangy aspect of the men, made it look as though there had been an unlikely suburban commute from Scarsdale to the land of Owen Wister. The men—masons from Beersheba, bank tellers from Haifa, curtain manufacturers from Tel Aviv—were all dressed in highly personal variations on the army uniform. In an army where no officer may order his men to charge, but only to follow him, there is a great deal of informality. "Tell my mother I am beautiful in my uniform," a soldier helping the civilians of Nir Yitzhak harvest peaches said to a visitor from home. But, without any actual battle eagerness, the general attitude seemed to be "What are they waiting for?" and "Let's get it over with.". . .

On Sunday, June 4th, a number of soldiers—a tenth of the army, according to some estimates—were given a day's leave, and several of the North African soldiers (sometimes referred to euphemistically as the Southern French) took advantage of their leave to return for a day to their families in the port of Elath. Elath seemed confident that war would not break out there. In the first place, people said, the port was now too strongly fortified, and, in the second, at the first sign of trouble the soldiers would blow up the neighboring port of Aqaba, Jordan's only outlet to the sea. In tents all along the beach, near the empty resort hotels, was the remnant of an international collection of waifs and strays with long hair and guitars whom one now finds in so many unlikely places, and who had long been making Elath a beatnik nomad's rendezvous. When they needed food, they scrounged it from the local citizens or from the army. When they needed money, they presented themselves in the morning at a café called Leon's, where they were recruited to dig trenches or to work for a day in King Solomon's Mines. At night, they gathered in a discothèque called the Half Past Midnight (where there were also several African students who had been stranded in Elath when their passage home through the Gulf had been postponed by the blockade). Asked why the nomads had not taken the advice of their various embassies and left the port, a long-haired guitar player from Stuttgart looked up cheerfully and said, *"Was? Wenn es grad lustig wird?* [What! When it's just getting lively?]" (Soldiers emplaning on a civilian flight from Elath to Tel Aviv were asked to check their guns in the cargo section.)

On Sunday night, at Rehovoth, the professors' wives were just completing their course in how to render assistance at the

Kaplan Hospital if war should break out. The cement walls of the still uncompleted building in which they met were lined with stretchers and sawhorses to put the stretchers on. The women were issued forms, in duplicate, on which they could check off a doctor's diagnosis, and thereby save him the time of writing things down himself. The lecturer, normally a gynecologist, warned the women that even to a seasoned medical man a casualty of war looks different from any other sort of patient. After the first four hours, he assured them, they would get used to it. He reviewed the forms with them, the ways of ascertaining the wounded man's identity (the pockets of civilian casualties, who did not, of course, have dog tags, would have to be searched) , and he went down the checklist for gravity of wounds—mild, medium, serious, mortal. There were several questions about the word "mortal." The doctor had used the wrong word in Hebrew—one meaning "mortal" in the sense of "human being." The matter was soon cleared up. One of the women crouched on the floor with her hands locked behind her head to show the position her daughter in kindergarten had been taught to adopt in case of bombing. " 'This is how the bunny sits,' she told me," the woman said. " 'See the bunny ears?' "

Late Saturday night, the Army informed the civilian guard at Rehovoth that they might let up on the security watch.

A Remote Conflict

On Monday, June 5th, at 8 A.M., the air-raid sirens went off all over Israel, and everyone knew that the country was at war. In one of the bomb shelters at the Institute, five languages were being spoken, with absolute calm, by scientists, children, visitors, and maids. A few minutes later, the all clear sounded, and everyone went to work, as though it were an ordinary day. General Dayan's voice came over the radio, speaking to the troops and announcing that tank battles were taking place at that moment in the Negev. *"Attaque à l'aube* [attack at dawn]," one of the scientists said as he walked to his laboratory. "That's good for us. It means that we've got the rising sun in the east behind us. In the Negev, the sun is pretty blinding.". . .

Tel Aviv, on the first afternoon of the war, was not much changed, except that all windows had been taped in accordance with instructions delivered over Kol Yisroel. Word had come that several *kibbutzim* along the Gaza Strip were being shelled, that Ein Gev, near the Syrian frontier, was under fire, that Haifa and Jerusalem were being attacked, and that for some reason the resort of Nethanya and the Arab village of Safad were being bombed. People seemed most worried about the civilian population of Jerusalem. An English translation of Dayan's speech to the troops was broadcast, announcing that the Arabs were being supported from Kuwait to Algeria. "I need not tell you," he added, in brief remarks to the civilian population, "that we are a small people but a courageous one. . . ."

On Tuesday morning at five, in Tel Aviv, there was an air-raid alarm (it turned out to have been a mistake) ; there had been none during the night. Bus service to Jerusalem was almost normal, except that, on account of Israeli army emplacements, buses had to make a detour of several kilometers through En Karem. On one bus, Kol Yisroel was audible, and, looking over into Jordan from the highway, one could see smoke rising from a town on Jordan's wedge into Israel and verify the report that Israeli troops were taking Latrun. Because Jerusalem had been shelled throughout the night (the Egyptian general, who, under the terms of the Hussein-Nasser pact, had been put in charge of Jordan's army, had often in the past expressed his belief in the shelling of civilians, since it diverted troops to their defense) , and was still being shelled by day, most of the population of the city was in shelters. Israeli troops were attacking gun emplacements in the Old City, taking care to observe the order to preserve the monuments of all faiths, if possible. The King David Hotel had incurred minor damage—a tree down, a few

broken windows, some slight injuries to members of the staff
—but Avram Zvi, who had been called up, was now wearing
a uniform and seemed enormously gratified. In the streets
outside, a few helmeted civilians and some restless little boys
kept telling one another to walk close to the walls and to run
across streets leading toward Jordan. From several directions,
there was the sound of machine-gun and mortar fire. In the
early afternoon, three journalists walked into the government
press office and were received with cheers. Accredited to Jordan, they had been stationed in the Old City, unable to file
copy, for several days. When the Israeli troops came, they had
simply walked across into the New City to file their copy
there. Then they walked back again. It was announced that
General Dayan had had tea on Mount Scopus that morning.

Sometime in the course of Tuesday, an army official called
a meeting of intellectuals in an office in Tel Aviv. He had in-
vited delegates from Rehovoth, from Technion, from the
Academy, and from the Hebrew University in Jerusalem.
(Because of the peculiar configuration of the shelling at that
hour, the professors from Jerusalem were unable to attend.)
He wanted to ask their advice on a number of questions, and
to brief them on the progress of the war. The war was suc-
ceeding so far beyond the most optimistic expectations that
there were problems that must be faced at once. The entire
Egyptian army had been mobilized at the front when the war
began, but Israel had spent the tense waiting period retrain-
ing reserves and repairing machinery, and the Egyptian air
force had been destroyed in the first hours of Monday morning. Apparently misled by the true reports over Kol Yisroel
that many Israeli border settlements had been attacked, and
by the false reports from the Voice of Thunder in Cairo that
Beersheba had been taken and that Tel Aviv was in flames,
King Hussein of Jordan—to the surprise and special regret of
Israel—had entered the war by noon, and in the afternoon
the Jordanian air force was destroyed as well. The Syrians,
originally the country most rabidly committed to the immediate extermination of Israel, were apparently enraged by

the reconciliation between Nasser and Hussein, whom Damascus was still determined to overthrow. Syria had entered the war by degrees throughout the day, and by nightfall the Syrian air force was destroyed. Fighting was going well on the ground on all fronts, and the problem was where to stop. Hussein, it seemed, was powerless to forbid the shelling of Jerusalem by Jordanian troops under Egyptian command, so it would be necessary for the Israelis to take the Old City. (The Rockefeller Institute, containing the Dead Sea Scrolls, the army spokesman announced, smiling ironically at the particular stir of interest that this aroused in his scholarly audience, had already been captured.) It was clear that Jerusalem could not be divided again. Would it be a good idea to announce plans to internationalize the Old City *before* it was completely in Israeli hands? There was another problem, he went on: Captured Egyptian documents, which had been translated only the night before, revealed that Nasser was far more seriously committed to the destruction of Israelis as *Jews,* and far more taken with the old Nazi programs, than had been supposed; plans, on the Nazi model, had been drawn up for the time after Israel's defeat. The question was whether to release these documents. What Israel wanted from this war, after all, was a lasting peace with its Arab neighbors. The two primary obstacles to this peace were the problems of Palestine and the Arab refugees. These problems could be solved. What purpose would be served in humiliating an already defeated Arab people by revealing the plans its leader may have had for destroying civilians? The question was discussed, inconclusively, for some time. Finally, the spokesman raised a question that had been puzzling the administration: What had happened to Egypt's missiles? Were the ones shown so often on parade merely dummies? He mentioned other possibilities: mechanical failure, fear of a mythical superweapon at Rehovoth, or pressure from Moscow to avoid what would have been purely futile destruction of cities. This led him to another matter: The Russians were not famous for their loyalty to losers, and the Arabs had lost. Was there any point in approaching the Russians now—or, at least, the Rumanians, who had declared themselves in such moderate terms? Several professors of Russian descent expressed themselves emotionally on the prospect of a *rapprochement* with their native land, but the others seemed skeptical. Certain questions, the spokesman said, in concluding the discussion (several professors present had to return to their laboratories or their military units), would simply be resolved by events, but, he said, "We will settle for nothing but peace this time.". . .

Tuesday Evening

Kol Yisroel reported, with the understatement that it was to display throughout the war, that fighting had now penetrated to the Egyptian side of the Sinai border. (In fact, Gaza had fallen, and soldiers were already beginning to find pairs and clusters of boots in the desert, which, they knew from the 1956 Sinai campaign, meant that the Egyptians were in barefoot rout.) The Jerusalem *Post* for the day, in mentioning the fact that casualties were beginning to come into Israeli hospitals, and that all of them were patient and brave, did not neglect to mention a soldier who, with one eye shot away and the other damaged, was as brave as the rest. He was a Jordanian legionnaire, the *Post* reported, and he kept repeating the only Hebrew words he knew: "We are brothers. We are brothers."

Someone mentioned that a Hebrew idiom for Arabs is "cousins," or "sons of our uncle," and that although the connotation was slightly pejorative, it need not always be that way. Someone praised the bravery, in particular, of the Jordanian legionnaires.

"I really think the reason we fight better is because we have no hinterland," Yoram [a young volunteer] said. "We can't swim to America. We simply have nowhere else to go." He left . . . and went into the moonlight, to begin his courier duty. "A perfect night for bombing," he said, looking into the clear sky. But there were no alarms at all that night.

On Wednesday morning, the casualties began pouring out of buses into the Kaplan Hospital, where the Rehovoth wives were waiting to work. . . . The wounded were silent, and as each stretcher was brought in it was immediately surrounded by many volunteers of both sexes, solicitous of the comfort of the wounded man. It turned out that among those critically wounded on the previous day was the son of the gynecologist who had had difficulty with the word "mortal" three nights before. "For us, you know, the army, it isn't an anonymous thing," someone remarked. "To us, everyone killed at the front is a tragedy."

LETTER FROM CAIRO [3]

Our ship arrived at Piraeus late this afternoon—46 hours after leaving Egypt. The sun is setting now; my room at the Athens Hilton offers a marvelous view of the Acropolis, but I'm too damn exhausted to think of sightseeing. I won't attempt to organize these notes on the Six-Day War, primarily because I suspect that the real story is on the Israeli side. The best thing to do, I think, is to provide you with a personalized Sit-Rep [situation report]—call it a Cairo Diary.

I arrived in Egypt on Saturday, June 3. After checking in at the Nile Hilton, I went to the United States Embassy for a briefing, got my U.A.R. press credentials from the information department and set up interviews for Monday. After lunch I set out to explore the city in a rickety taxi. The heat was oppressive. My driver kept mopping his brow with what once might have been a clean white shirt. In the past few years I've been in some fairly grubby places but I was totally unprepared for the stench and filth of Cairo—flies everywhere, men sleeping on the sidewalks, buzzards circling overhead. We followed the traffic into the Mussky, the central bazaar.

[3] From "Letter from Cairo," by Trevor Armbrister, manager of Washington bureau. *Saturday Evening Post.* 240:62-3. Jl. 29, '67. Reprinted by permission of the author.

Men in flowing galabias were shouting at every corner. The walls were ablaze with the pictures of Nasser and posters urging the destruction of Israel. The most common of these depicted two large Arab boots squashing a tiny figure wearing the Star of David.

Nasser had declared the first military alert on May 15. For the past two weeks there had been continual air-raid drills, but to say that an atmosphere of impending crisis hung over the city would be an exaggeration. Most Egyptians seemed to think the crisis was over, that Nasser had won a major victory by blockading the Gulf of Aqaba without having to fire a shot. Vice President Zakarria Moheiddin was in Algiers that Saturday and was scheduled to fly to Washington in a few days to confer with President Johnson. The English-language newspaper *Egyptian Mail* ran a banner headline reading MORE INTERNATIONAL SUPPORT FOR THE ARAB CAUSE. Mohammed Heikal, editor of *Al Ahram* and confidant of Nasser, declared, "If Israel strikes to break the Arab blockade, she will be shattered." Heikal was sure, as were most of the people around Nasser, that the United States and Britain would persuade the Israelis not to attack.

But what if an attack did come? The Egyptians seemed equally confident that their modern, 400-plane air force (including at least 150 late-model MIG 21's) could wipe the Israeli Mirages and Mystères from the sky. Egyptian ground forces had already taken up their advance position in Sinai.

On Sunday, June 4, the *Egyptian Gazette* headlined the news that private talks to end the Aqaba blockade had failed. Army commander General Abdul Mortaga issued a message to his troops which began:

Brave fighters, the decisive historical moment which our Arab nation is passing through today is centered around the sacred battle which you will fight to restore the usurped rights of the Arabs. . . .

Workers piled sandbags in front of the radio-television building. Still, there was an air of unreality about all these warlike pronouncements and preparations. The swimming pool at the Nile Hilton was crowded.

The War Begins

On Monday morning I was awakened early by the rattling of the hotel's windows. It was a clear, crisp (for Cairo) morning; a few feluccas were sailing slowly down the Nile. The rattling, I decided, was just the wind. I called room service and asked for breakfast. "We cannot serve any food now," the operator said. "We are being bombed." I looked out the window again. I could see flashes in the direction of the airport, but I could see no planes. The elevators weren't functioning, so I ran down the stairs to the lobby. I joined a group of reporters and raced to the radio-television center five blocks away on the Nile Corniche. At every corner, small groups of Egyptians huddled around transistor radios. "It begins," one of them told me, his face a mixture of pride and anxiety— "the war."

The TV building was mobbed. Moments after we showed up, Kamal Bakr, the U.A.R.'s pudgy, quietly unprofessional press-relations chief, tacked military communiqué No. 1 on the bulletin board. "Israel began its aggression this morning," the document read, "by raiding Cairo and now the governorates (sic) in the U.A.R. The U.A.R. military crafts face the planes." Communiqué No. 2 at 10:20 told us that Radio Tel Aviv had just announced an Egyptian air raid on the city. Ten minutes later the Middle East News Agency ticker announced that twenty-three Israeli planes had been shot down. Pandemonium. The crowds outside the building began chanting "Nasser, Nasser" and hamming for American TV crews. A group of white-uniformed police marched past the TV building. Their leaders carried stubby Czech-made submachine guns. The rest of the men carried broomsticks.

At 11:10, press officer Bakr told us that forty-two—not twenty-three—Israeli planes had been shot down in the first attack. The U.A.R., he added, had not lost a single plane. Furthermore, the Israeli bombs had inflicted no damage. Five minutes later an air-raid siren wailed for the third time that morning. I saw one bomb burst off to the west, then looked up to see the contrails of what was presumably an Israeli jet zigzagging at high altitude. A little while later, that estimate of Israeli losses was adjusted again, this time to ninety planes. Great whooping and cheering. Radio Cairo began broadcasting messages in Hebrew. Arab armies would be in Tel Aviv tomorrow night.

Even in retrospect it's hard to explain the Arab claims. Surely, by this time, the Arab commanders must have realized that they had already lost. The demolition of the U.A.R. air force had been complete. How could they have been caught napping so badly? They had Russian radar. There is talk that they just forgot to turn on their sets.

Moods Change

And yet from our vantage point—or lack of one—we could see nothing to indicate that the war was going badly for the Arabs. The military communiqués kept flowing into the press center—each one couched in superlatives. That night we heard our first news from the outside world. The BBC reported that Israeli troops were advancing deep into Sinai. BBC also quoted a Tel Aviv report that two Egyptian jets had got into a dogfight and shot each other down.

At 2:40 Tuesday morning we were hustled out of bed and escorted to the lobby by civil-defense workers in blue pajamas. A few flashes in the distance, an occasional barr-umph, some sporadic ack-ack fire. This went on several times that night, moving one American to proclaim that he was going to move his cot into the closet just to escape the air-raid wardens. All of us were down in the lobby again at eight. The breakfast room was closed. Israeli planes were approaching, the bell captain said. We hustled up to the TV center. Even at this hour, the loudspeakers on every corner were blaring, "*Idrib, Idrib, Idrib*"—strike, strike, strike.

On Tuesday morning a banner headline in *Al Akhbar* announced, OUR ARMOURED FORCES ADVANCE DEEPLY INSIDE THE ENEMY LINES. The English-language *Egyptian Gazette* ran a similar head and an inside shot of what appeared to be a piece of scrap iron. The caption read, "Wreckage of the wicked raider." The *Gazette*'s horoscope column advised readers to "take action along technical lines if you would realize better than average gains today." The Egyptians should have paid heed.

Almost overnight, the mood of the city changed. The atmosphere was becoming increasingly anti-Western. The second air raid of the day began at 9:05. A few minutes later the MENA [Middle East News Agency] ticker in the TV center chattered out a communiqué marked "urgent, urgent."

It has been definitely proved [the report stated], that the United States and Britain are participating in the Israeli military aggression. Some U.S. and British aircraft carriers are undertaking large-scale activities in supporting Israel. . . .

Dan Garcia of the U.S. embassy staff promptly tacked a press release on the bulletin board, denying the charge as a "total fabrication." As a group gathered around it, press officer Bakr tore down Garcia's denial.

Most of us had asked Bakr repeatedly for a briefing from the U.A.R. military types. We'd also asked to see the downed Israeli planes and inspect the bombing damage. Now Bakr declared that there would be no briefings, and we were ordered not to try to go off on our own. Later that morning, a Land Rover pulled alongside us in the street, and a man in the front seat spit at us. As we went back to the hotel, we noticed that the police guard in front of the U.S. compound had been doubled.

By midafternoon on Tuesday it was clear that a U.S.-U.A.R. break was imminent. Nasser had to break diplomatic relations to give credence to his claim of Western intervention. At eight o'clock—during an air raid—Kamal Bakr rushed into the hotel cafeteria. He came to the table where several newsmen were eating and said, "I have very important news." We asked him to join us for dinner. "It is impossible," Bakr replied. "You have to leave the country—tonight." How were we supposed to go? Call your embassy, Bakr said. We did, and an officer there told us to stay put for the time being, at least. Later that night, air-raid sirens wailed again. A frightened child began to cry. I could see flashes and heard loud explosions from the direction of the Pyramids [three large pyramids at Giza, near Cairo]. The Egyptians were replying with rockets and ack-ack fire. They didn't seem to hit anything.

On Wednesday morning, despair settled over the city. Sails were lowered on the few feluccas traveling the Nile. Shortly after noon, all twenty-two American reporters were rounded up and sent to the Nile Hotel, a dingy establishment facing the Corniche. As we milled about the entrance, a convoy of army vehicles rumbled past loaded with sandbags and artillery shells. We'd seen such convoys before, and the troops had always been singing. Now they were silent. The Egyptians made it clear that we were under house arrest. A blue-gowned Nubian named Mahatma guarded the hotel entrance, thrusting a thick black arm in front of anyone who attempted even to peer outside.

The hotel's restaurant had shifted its service to the boiler room, a smelly cavern abuzz with flies. The luncheon menu Wednesday was equally unappetizing, the *pièce de résistance* being a dried piece of meat which we decided came from a camel. Waiters in filthy galabias plopped six bottles of beer on the table. There would be no more until the war was over; the beer factory was closed.

Two reporters in our group had short-wave radios. We spent our time listening to BBC and VOA [Voice of America] and wondering how long our internment would last. There was another air raid that night and the city was blacked out again. From our windows, we could see a thin cordon of Egyptian cavalry posted near the hotel entrance. They looked decidedly unmilitary.

The headline in the *Egyptian Gazette* Thursday morning read, ARAB FORCES INFLICT BIG LOSSES ON ISRAELIS. According to the BBC Thursday morning, Jordan decided to accept the cease-fire. The Israelis had reached the banks of the Suez Canal. Radio Cairo declared only that U.A.R. forces had regrouped at Sharm el Sheikh and that they had annihilated a regiment of Israeli paratroopers. Throughout the day loudspeakers kept up the incessant din of martial music.

Nasser Speaks

At noon on Friday we received word that Nasser would address his people that evening for the first time since the start of the war. Someone located a TV set and at 7:30 we gathered around it. Nasser looked exhausted. He spoke in soft tones and began by admitting that the U.A.R. had suffered a "grievous setback." The Israeli attack, he said, "came with much more force than we expected and with much more than the enemy owns. It is clear that there were other powers behind the enemy. . . ." And on into a reiteration of the charge that America and Britain were involved. He told his people that they had to "insist upon the removal of the effects of the aggression, learn a lesson from the setback (he never called it a defeat) and maintain a unified attitude." Just at that moment, an air-raid siren wailed. Nasser went on: "I have decided to give up completely any official or political post. . . ." The entire address lasted twenty-four minutes and there were tears in Nasser's eyes at the end. To me, it was all very convincing.

The chants began less than twenty minutes later. From all over the city you could hear "Nasser, Nasser, Nasser." The voices got louder and louder, and someone reminded us that an Iraqi mob had dragged Europeans from their hotels in Baghdad in 1956 and butchered them in the streets. Suddenly the sky lit up in an eerie display. The crazy Egyptians were firing ack-ack and rockets at the stars—and some of the bursts seemed close. A few minutes later, an army captain shouted, "Rush to your rooms. They are coming," and up we went. At 10, we were escorted back downstairs for dinner. A few demonstrators, someone explained, had tried to set fire to the hotel, but they had been stopped by the police.

At 1:20 Saturday morning, just minutes after most of us had dozed off, we were awakened. United States embassy officials expected trouble in the morning. So did Egyptian security officials. We would leave the hotel at once. They loaded us into gray prison vans and at 3 A.M. drove us under guard to the railroad station. As we waited for the baggage to be loaded, a mob of about 5,000 on its way back to the city from Nasser's residence passed within two blocks of us. Our train, which was surprisingly comfortable, arrived in Alexandria at 8 A.M. We were led past rows of machine-gun-carrying soldiers into a Mussolini-Modern terminal building.

We were forced to hand over all Egyptian currency. One particularly venal inspector reached into the wallet of an embassy secretary and extracted two hundred dollars. The girl protested, then asked a senior U.S. diplomat to intercede. He just shrugged his shoulders helplessly. There was really nothing he could do. One American scientist was pushed up against a wall and frisked for the crime of having been born in Palestine, Texas.

The Greek ship Carina II had been in Alexandria harbor for some time, but the Egyptians didn't allow us on board until 4 P.M.—eight foodless hours after our arrival at the terminal. We sailed at six o'clock. As we left the harbor, two Egyptian submarines which had been following us submerged. What a relief it was to be aboard that ship—even if it meant spending the next two nights in an uncomfortable deck chair, which it did. And what a group we were: Among the 557 bedraggled Americans were a man who X-rays pyramids, a ninety-three-year-old judge, the world's foremost authority on ticks, one Argentine Jew and four Canadian beatniks. The cost of the voyage was $78.20, and our method of payment must have set a precedent. Never before have refugees been able to pay for an evacuation with a credit card.

I left Egypt feeling a mixture of anger and pity toward the Egyptians. Once again, after "unresigning," Nasser has managed to turn defeat to his own advantage and his position seems safe—but only for the moment. There was an abortive military coup last year. There were further rumblings in the army this spring, and it's likely that these rumblings will increase in volume when all the barefoot and beaten soldiers get back to Cairo from Sinai. Every expert with whom I talked expects internal strife within six months. Egypt's economy is a shambles and it is bound to get worse.

EGYPT TODAY [4]

Nationalism is more than ever the dominant theme in Egyptian political life this spring. The consciously expressed concern not to be engulfed in any alien system either of imperialism or of international communism is insistent and genuine. Soviet military experts are in Egypt only "for specific periods," writes editor Mohammed Hassanein Heikal in *Al Ahram*. They will not be allowed to dominate the state, but, he explains, Egypt is in great need of specific aspects of military training, which Soviet technicians are now providing.

In fact, a Russian version of Military Assistance Group such as the United States has long deployed in Asia now exists in Egypt. It involves an estimated 4,000 officers and engineers. They have come along with the simpler, mostly defensive Russian weapons which have restocked Egyptian arsenals since last summer. When it became apparent that a peasant army could not master the intricacies of sophisticated weapons, and that their officers showed a fatal lack of understanding and initiative in desert warfare, Egypt appealed for basic training as well as arms.

Russia in Warm Water

The Russian presence is pervasive but not conspicuous. Egypt's defeat provided the opening for the Soviets to move into the planning of defense; for the easy negotiation of landing rights for Russian planes at Cairo West, Alexandria,

[4] From a report on Egypt. *Atlantic.* 221:10+. Ap. '68. Copyright © 1968, by The Atlantic Monthly Company, Boston, Mass. Reprinted with permission.

Luxor, and Aswan, and for port facilities for the Soviet fleet at Alexandria and Port Said. Russia has reached the warm water at last. It is in the Mediterranean to stay.

Economic bonds between Moscow and Cairo are also strong. Trade between them has reached an annual figure of $243 million. Among the items coming into Egypt are 300,000 tons of wheat and much industrial equipment. From Czechoslovakia and East Germany, Egypt has ordered a total of thirty complete flour mills. From the Egyptian side, cotton, rice, textiles, and agricultural products will be exported to the Soviet Union.

Russians have been the all-important partners in the Aswan High Dam, from which cheap power now reaches as far as Tahrir Province, north of Cairo. The High Dam is nearing completion, holding back some 40 million cubic meters of water and altering the society and economy of the Nile region completely. The High Dam Ministry estimates that the dam has already saved $150 million by preventing flood damage. Much planning has accompanied the dam's building. Development of a new diversified industrial complex at Aswan awaits funds. This is being done under the auspices of the Regional Planning of Aswan office, under the governorate of Aswan. It has had as consultants experts on small industry from the Ford Foundation and is now receiving further help from the UN Development Program.

Meanwhile, newly irrigated land reclaimed from the desert already produces two cotton crops or three cereal crops where only one crop was possible after normal Nile floods. Altogether the dam will increase Egypt's arable land by one sixth and its agricultural output by one quarter.

Tough Line

In spite of the enormous Soviet financial investment in Egypt over the last ten years, political relations between the two nations are undefined. There is no mutual defense treaty, although in the shock of defeat last summer President Nasser wanted one. Without Moscow's material and political support the effects of the defeat would have been catastrophic for Egypt. Given these, Cairo can maintain a tough line in relation to Israel and reassert some of its influence in the Arab world. That influence survives. In recognition of it the Israelis publicly say that no peace treaty without Nasser's agreement would be worth having.

Soviet diplomats find it impossible, however, to influence Cairo's decisions directly on the Palestine question. They failed to win acceptance of a moderate solution last summer at the UN. They remain unable to alter the government's position on the Suez Canal, or on its hope of reestablishing diplomatic relations with Washington. Rather cautiously they have been comparing Nasser's "bourgeois" regime with that of the more radical Boumedienne in Algeria. *Pravda's* Igor Belyayev in a long article in February [1968] wrote:

> Even in nationalist Egyptian circles there are fairly open proponents of an all-around *rapprochement* with the United States. These people try to convince themselves that only the Americans are in the position to solve the Middle East crisis. . . . A very perfidious design is hidden in such claims. It is a question of the most genuine capitulation before imperialism. Carry out the design of the American lobbyists in Cairo, and the United States would be able to rely on those changes which would favor its monopoly capitalism and reduce to naught the gains of the Egyptian revolution.

The *Pravda* article reflects a general concern among the Egyptian hierarchy that their posture of nonalignment will be impossible to maintain unless better relations with the West are cultivated. It was for this reason that they were so eager to restore relations with Great Britain last fall. They tried energetically, and have succeeded in retaining their oil contracts with two U.S. companies—Pan American in the Red Sea region, and Phillips Petroleum in the western desert. Within a year of the formation of a joint company with Pan American the Morgan field has reached a production of 100,000 barrels a day, thus offsetting the loss of the Sinai fields captured by Israel. This oil is now being processed at British Petroleum's refinery at Aden, pending the complete restoration of the Suez refineries damaged in October. This spring Egypt's third productive field at El Alamein will add 30,000 barrels a day.

Official interpretation of the value of these finds emphasizes their political aspect. As the government spokesman, Dr. Mohammed H. El-Zayyat, put it, more Egyptian oil will help Egypt to resist pressure from any side, to remain independent. In terms of money, oil income helps to rescue Egypt from the near bankruptcy brought on by Suez Canal closure and loss of tourism.

Political Traffic

These economic developments add a new dimension to Egypt's future. It ceases to be a have-not country and can anticipate means of carrying out its ambitious industrial plans. Planning is now in the hands of Dr. Abdel Moneim Kaissouny, one of the country's ablest financial figures. His reemergence in the cabinet is a sign of the regime's desire to reestablish itself in the international financial marketplace. One of the most promising projects under discussion between Egyptian planners and a British engineering firm is for a large oil pipeline to bypass the Suez Canal. The pipeline would have an initial capacity of 50 million tons a year and would link the Gulf of Suez with Port Said or Alexandria. It is asserted that use of the line would be less expensive than enlarging the Suez Canal to take giant modern tankers.

Aside from the technical advantages of a new pipeline, its construction would diminish the symbolic importance of the canal. Nationalization of the canal made President Nasser a hero in the Arab world in 1956. It has always carried a heavy freight of political traffic. It was for this reason that Israel fought to use it. The amount of Israeli-flag shipping which could use it is small, but the sensitivity of both countries on this issue is acute.

Thus when Egypt started under United Nations auspices to survey the canal in January in order to free fifteen ships blocked there since last June, Israel insisted on being consulted at every step. When it became obvious that Egypt could physically clear the canal at its northern end without Israeli interference, because Israel does not occupy the eastern bank on the last five miles at the northern end, Israel protested. This put it in the position of denying clearance of the blocked ships for its own political reasons. No amount of reasoning or reassurance by United Nations officials and observers that this was to be a one-time operation, not a reopening of the canal to traffic, could budge Israel. Egypt then stopped all attempts to free the ships. It could simply wait until the nine countries involved as owners of the ships exerted more pressure for clearance.

Cairo's Credit

In this case Egypt was in the position to claim that a technical service was in the general interest and therefore above politics. This has been a familiar argument in Israel for many years—when swamps in demilitarized zones in the north adjoining Syria were drained, for example, to make them productive. But on the canal, where Israel now patrols the eastern bank for all but the northern five-mile stretch, the Israelis remain transfixed by the prospect of joining in its traffic at last.

On the Egyptian side, it has taken considerable persuasion by international interests to convince Egyptian planners that it is in their best interest to establish an alternative to the canal. They have accepted the idea and begun to shift their interest to it, encouraged by international petroleum companies in the Arabian Gulf. But before any new large projects can be carried out in Egypt, it will be necessary to reestablish Egyptian credit standing. The government has been trying to reschedule its large debts to foreign commercial banks. Most important is regularization of its standing with the International Monetary Fund, with which it is in default in the amount of some $50 million. European commercial banks have been more responsive to Egyptian requests for short-term loans than have American banks. Ever since the Yemeni war and its threat to the stability of the

Arabian peninsula, American institutions have been increasingly cool to Egyptian appeals for funds.

The Men from Moscow

At this stage Egyptian planners must therefore reckon without American help in any field except education. The American presence on the Egyptian scene has never been so slight. Today the small contingent of diplomats who staff the American Interests Section of the Spanish Embassy stick to their technical tasks. They observe the novel activities of a whole new breed of Soviet diplomats who ornament the Cairo social scene. The Russian ambassador, Serge Vinogradov, has become the most sought-after and honored guest at state functions. He is backstopped by about a thousand Russians speaking good English and Egyptian Arabic. The women of the contingent have dropped the uncaring styles of the past for the latest European modes. On the surface they have replaced the banished Europeans of another age.

Mr. Vinogradov has easy access to President Nasser, and likes to appear as the president's mentor. Still, government decisions so far have not followed an all-out anti-Western line. And within the Egyptian official family there is known to be much anxiety at the preponderant role assumed by the men from Moscow.

The generation of technocrats which keeps Egypt from civil chaos grew up under British and French tutelage. Their leaders studied at London School of Economics and the Sorbonne or at Harvard. They are at home in the Western world, are nostalgic for contact with it, and angry that much of it refuses to see the justice of their position on Arab unity under Egypt, and on Israel. They are also weary of responsibility in a hectic period of revolution; and some of them have found a way out by joining international services via the United Nations. Today it is possible for more of these elite to leave if they choose. Late in the fall of 1967 the government decided that Egyptian families could emigrate legally, taking with them their household possessions and some

cash. There has been an exodus of both Christians and Muslims in the last six months. Many go to Canada, some to the
United States. They represent a new kind of loss for Egypt,
of educated and skilled professionals, discouraged with their
position and anxious for the future. If the tide of such emigration increases, it will be a sign that the regime can no
longer offer real hope to the educated class.

Dr. Kaissouny has underscored the lack of educated manpower in a report on employment prospects up to 1975. He
predicts a shortage of candidates for managerial and technical posts of some 30,000 by 1970. The supply of intermediate
technical trainees will be short 160,000 candidates. The implications for development of the economy are obvious.

Egypt has not yet dealt with the great technological gap
exposed by its military defeat last summer. But Russian advisers have not spared feelings in putting much of the military failure down to lack of training. Dr. Kaissouny is saying
that there will be as fatal a gap in preparation for industrialization if technical education is not improved and increased.

Much United Nations technical help has been sought by
the government in this field. UNESCO and the International
Labour Organisation have helped to set standards and teach
teachers of vocational training. There has been help on training for civil aviation, for railway workers, and for industrial
management. The UN Development Program is concentrat-
ing on aiding projects for draining irrigated land, a necessity
as more acreage comes under perennial irrigation from the
High Dam. It is also advising on mineral development of the
Aswan region and on new industries which can be developed
as the power grid begins to extend across the country.

Such help adds up in the over-all development effort. But
what strikes the Western observer is the shortage of education
for industry in a country which envisions salvation through
industrialization. This shortage, plus an artificial one caused
by the removal of many talented managerial people for political reasons, threatens the country's economic future.
There is as yet no mobilization of talent, much of it still

available in the country. The Israeli war does not seem to have had the Sputnik-like effect it might have had in directing energies to Egypt's technical deficiencies.

Political Impasse

As time passes without a resolution of the political impasse with Israel, Egypt's terms have not softened. Cairo has made what it considers its best offer. This is for demilitarization of both sides of the Sinai frontier after withdrawal of Israeli forces; submission of the Tiran strait question to the International Court, with open passage meanwhile; return of Palestinians to their land in the West Bank, at least, in exchange for Israeli passage through the canal; and negotiations through the Mixed Armistice Commission, which continues to exist in spite of Israel's ten-year boycott of it. The Egyptians believe they have taken "a giant step" in admitting Israel's right to exist. They say they have been talking directly with Israel through the MAC since 1949, that this is the best way for negotiations to be held, and that they cannot concede more. They do not claim Gaza but are concerned with its refugee population, of whom some 12,000 single males are being sheltered on a small dole in Egypt. There is no work for them, and only a few are qualified for university training. . . . In the long run the Arabs have high cards. But in the short run, Israel, with its strong Western political support and brilliant advocacy, may have the votes. They are paper votes, however, and will not force the direct talks Israel says it wants.

Any conventional interpretation of last summer's Arab defeat would have predicted Nasser's downfall, Egypt's economic collapse, and perhaps the West Bank and Jordan working arrangements with Israel. None of the seers would have guessed that the two oil monarchies under chronic attack from Cairo, Saudi Arabia and Libya, would be sending Egypt a cash subsidy to keep it going all year; or that all the NATO countries of the Mediterranean basin would stand behind the Arabs and keep open the door to the East which Moscow so eagerly rushed to close.

Looking at Egypt today it is possible to see either peace or war ahead. The new Russian weaponry may be largely defensive and may provide the backdrop of defensive power needed before any government can approach a settlement with Israel. The Russians clearly favor a settlement but do not have the power to influence it politically. Somewhat inconsistently, the Egyptians and all other Arabs greatly overestimate the influence of the United States on Israel. It is no exaggeration to say that we have never had less influence in Tel Aviv.

BITTER VICTORY [5]

Morally—and politically—there can be no doubt that right triumphed in the Arab-Israeli war this summer. Connoisseurs of the Arab mentality sometimes suggest that when President Nasser threatened to "drive the Israelis into the sea" he did not mean what he said. The Israelis—who have good cause to remember that when dictators threaten genocide it is wise to take them seriously—could be forgiven for adopting a less philosophical view. But although the Israeli government had no choice but to act as it did, the brutal truth is that Israel cannot obtain the security she needs unless the Arabs are prepared to give it her; and any serious analysis of the situation must start from that unpalatable, but inescapable, fact. Even if the Israelis were prepared, in Professor Talmon's phrase to become "the Spartans of the Middle East" and to live by the sword instead of walking by the book, they lack the power to dictate a peace settlement against the wishes of those with whom they seek peace. And for Israel, anything less than a peace settlement is not merely a second-best, it is a disaster.

Some Israelis seem to imagine that even if Israel fails to come to terms with the Arabs, she can at least enjoy greater security than she enjoyed before the war, by virtue of her

[5] Article by David Marquand, Labour member of Parliament. *Encounter* (London). 30:31-3. F. '68. Reprinted by permission.

conquests on the West Bank, on the Syrian Heights and in the Sinai Desert. This notion is not merely false; it is a dangerous reversal of the truth. The fact is that if Israel fails to make peace with the Arabs she will be worse off than she was before the war. She will face an even more implacable enemy, even more determined to wipe out past humiliations, and even more prepared to pay whatever price may be asked for the wherewithal to do so.

Once this is accepted, however, Israel's current attitudes and behavior are more alarming than most Israelis seem to recognize. For if Israel can only obtain the kind of peace settlement she needs if the Arabs are prepared to let her have it, it follows that both sides—and not merely the side which lost the war—must be prepared to make concessions. In fact, however, Israel's behavior since the war has been the reverse of conciliatory; and on the crucial questions of the West Bank and the refugees it has been downright provocative. It is true that Israel cannot conceivably hand over the West Bank to Jordan without peace negotiations. The West Bank is the best bargaining counter she has ever had, or is ever likely to have; and she is entirely justified in retaining control of it until the Jordanians are willing to come to terms. But the success of this maneuver depends, by definition, on Israel's willingness to return the West Bank to Jordan when a peace settlement has been reached. Thus, any actions on Israel's part which are likely to give the Arabs grounds for suspecting that she intends to keep the West Bank for ever, and to use it as *Lebensraum* for Jewish settlement, are suicidally inept. And this, of course, is precisely what Israel has done.

At a deeper level, moreover, there is little sign that Israel is prepared psychologically for the adjustments which will be necessary if the Middle East is to enjoy a stable peace. It is clear that Israel cannot hope to live in peace with her neighbors unless they cease to regard her as an alien intruder and accept her as a Middle Eastern state like themselves. Any suggestion of this sort, however, is violently—sometimes hysterically—rejected by the vast majority of Israelis.

Israel [I was recently told, not once but a hundred times] is *not* a Middle Eastern state. We are Westerners, with a Western culture and a Western political system. We have no objection to carrying the blessings of Western technology and Western civilization to the more backward parts of the Middle East. But for God's sake don't ask us to become Middle Easterners ourselves. How would you like it if you were told to become West Indians?

The Alien State

These attitudes are understandable, if unattractive; but they bode ill for peace in the Middle East. The same applies to the even thornier question of Israel's psychological relationship with world Jewry. Most Israelis seem genuinely unable to realize that beneath the wild, illogical and sometimes nonsensical charges which the Arabs have brought against them, there does lie one uncomfortable kernel of truth. This kernel is, of course, the charge that Israel is not a state like any other, but the spearhead of a vast Zionist invasion of the Arab world: an alien bridgehead which is likely to expand inexorably until all the Jews of Diaspora are brought within its confines, unless its expansion is prevented by force. In a strictly factual sense, of course, this charge is absurd. Israel has been in existence for twenty years, and has attracted only a miserable trickle of immigrants from the one sizable Jewish community in the world whose members are free to leave— namely, the Jewish community of the United States. If this is the case in the 1960's, when large numbers of American Jews are still only partially assimilated, it is hardly likely to cease being the case at the end of the century, when the American Jewish community will be far more thoroughly assimilated into American society than it is now. But although the Arabs are mistaken to fear a great new influx of Jewish immigrants into Israel, they can be forgiven for making the mistake. For the Israelis make exactly the same mistake; and deny, with vehement passion, that it is a mistake at all.

The Zionist Ideal

The result is a perverse and tragic paradox. Israelis and Arabs both share the same misconception of the nature and destiny of the state of Israel: because they share it, they cannot make peace. Both believe that because Israel was founded by Zionists, it must remain Zionist. Both believe that because the starving and tortured Jews of postwar Europe had nowhere to go but Palestine, the increasingly assimilated Jews of North America will follow their example. Both believe that because the population of Israel is predominantly Jewish she cannot evolve into an ordinary secular state, in which Jews and Muslims, Christians and atheists, live side by side; owe their allegiance to the secular authorities rather than to any religious or ethnic community; and cease to concern themselves with the ethnic and religious affiliations of their fellow-citizens. In fact, these beliefs are false as well as dangerous. It is true that when Israel was founded it was necessary for her to develop an ideology capable of welding together a mass of immigrants from different cultures and social backgrounds. Since the only thing these immigrants had in common was their sense of being Jewish, it was inevitable that this ideology should have blurred the distinction between Jewishness and Israeli nationhood. But this does not alter the fact that the distinction exists, and that it is bound to become more and more pronounced. Most Jews outside Israel have no intention of going there to live, and their descendants will have less. As time goes on the barriers between the Jewish communities of the outside world, and the societies of which they form a part, will fade away until the difference between a Jew and a Gentile becomes no more portentous to either than the difference between an Anglican and a Methodist. Meanwhile, a new generation will have grown up in Israel. This new generation will know of the heroism and suffering of the present generation of Jews only from its history books; and it will have little in common with the increasingly un-Jewish Jews of the outside world.

These developments, moreover, are desirable as well as inevitable. Forcible assimilation, of the kind now practiced by the Soviet Union, is an evil since it entails discrimination and persecution. That is why it is unlikely to succeed. But voluntary assimilation, of the kind taking place inexorably in the United States and Britain, is a blessing—both to those who are being assimilated, and to the wider society into which they are assimilating themselves. This voluntary assimilation, however, is steadily undermining the ruling ideology of the Israeli state. Hence, of course, the violent indignation with which even moderate Israeli politicians deny that it is happening; and insist, in defiance of the evidence, that somewhere beyond the horizon lies the promise of a great new ingathering of the exiles which will finally realize the original Zionist dream. The paradox is that if these Israeli politicians were right, the future of Israel would indeed be hopeless. If Israel really were the bridgehead for a great Zionist invasion of the Middle East, the Arabs would be justified in fearing her and doing all they could to nip her expansionism in the bud.

Peace between Israel and the Arabs, in other words, is possible only because Zionism is wrong: and it will be probable only when Israel herself makes it clear that she realizes that Zionism is wrong. Everything else, it seems to me, depends on that. It is easy to sketch out the terms of a possible peace treaty. Israel obviously needs a guarantee of her *de jure* existence as a state, and frontier adjustments to give her greater military security. In return, she will obviously have to give back most of the occupied territories to their former owners; to allow back the refugees who fled from the West Bank this summer; to accept some status short of complete annexation for the old city of Jerusalem; and perhaps to arrange some form of compensation for the original refugees who fled from what is now Israel twenty years ago. But a peace treaty of this sort (or indeed of any sort) would not be worth the paper it was written on unless it were accompanied by a genuine decision on the part of the Arabs to accept Israel as a fact of Middle Eastern life—a decision guaranteed not by signatures on a treaty, but by a fundamental change of attitude. But no such change in the Arab attitude to Israel is possible, it seems to me, until an equivalent change has taken place in Israel's attitude to herself. At present, Israel sees herself as a Jewish state which happens to be situated in the Middle East. Permanent peace will not be possible until she sees herself as a Middle Eastern state, most of whose people happen to be Jews.

In the long run, this change seems certain to take place. The critical question is how long the run turns out to be.

THE ISRAELI OCCUPATION [6]

Nine months after the Six-Day War, the occupied territories are still a kind of popular sensation in Israel, a source of pride and a headache. For some, the occupation has proved that Jews can be as beastly as others; for others, it has proved the exact opposite. But for most Israelis, it has above all provided a seemingly inexhaustible tourist attraction. Hotels in the traditional vacation grounds of Israel—Elath, Haifa, and Safed—were half-empty last fall; bitterly complaining owners resorted to what is by now the almost automatic reaction of Israeli businessmen in trouble: an appeal to the government for subsidies.

But into the occupied areas of Hebron, Bethlehem, Nablus, Ramallah, and the Gaza Strip, Israelis pour by the tens of thousands on weekends and holidays. The military permit system, having broken down under the sheer weight of *protectsia* (Hebrew slang for "pull" or connections in high places), has been abolished altogether on the West Bank and in the Gaza Strip. There are still customs checkpoints, however; since Israel's extremely high import duties have not been levied in the occupied territories, returning cars are searched for television sets, English woolens, Japanese tape

[6] From article by Amos Elon, Israeli journalist and author of *Journey Through a Haunted Land. Commentary.* 45:41-7. Mr. '68. Reprinted from *Commentary*, by permission; copyright © 1968 by the American Jewish Committee.

recorders. But travel back and forth is free, upon presentation of an identity card or passport. One index of the extreme popularity of the occupied territories as a tourist attraction is the fact that Israeli tourism to Europe, on a sharp rise in recent years, diminished drastically in 1967. Only some 60,000 Israelis went abroad last year, as against more than 100,000 in 1966. On a nice weekend, by contrast, 30,000 Israelis will likely stream into East Jerusalem or drive through Samaria and Judea. A few thousand more can be found roaming about the Gaza Strip, exploring the vast wastes of the Sinai peninsula by jeep, or even venturing on the latest craze of them all: a week-long safari by camelback from the secluded fourth-century Greek Orthodox monastery of St. Catherine to the top of Mount Sinai, and from there southward to Sharm el-Sheikh, the route leading from one military outpost to the next, all hospitable but entirely ill-equipped for the purpose.

A few years ago, when Israeli tourists to Cyprus—hungry for consumer goods—bought up nearly all the electric irons and transistors on the island, a local humorist commented that Israelis are not merely travelers, they are traveling salesmen. Now, whether in uniform or mufti, they are not simply conquerors; they are also fanatic sightseers and eager shoppers at the bazaars of Hebron or Nablus. Shops on the West Bank are constantly replenishing their stock from dealers in Jordan, as semi-official trade across the Jordan River continues, undisturbed by—and sometimes in the midst of—frequent border incidents. But if Israelis do not behave like conquerors, they are not simply tourists either; rather, like embarrassed patriots, they can be observed in the attempt, undertaken without ease, and perhaps overoptimistically, to redraw in their minds the geographical borders of their country. Although by now they have done so several times, many still feel a bit of a sweet chill as they cross what civilians call "the borders of the state" and what in military jargon is known as "the green line." Why green? Perhaps because on most maps the borders of 1949 are marked in deep green, or per-

haps because the border really is green. On the Israeli side—
shady forests, artificially irrigated plantations, intensely cultivated fields, and above all, lawns, green, cool-looking, and
pleasing to the eye on a hot summer day. On the other side—
bare rock, poorly cultivated land, naked hilltops, and, above
all, virtually no trees. Further inland, to be sure, around
Hebron, or in Jericho and Nablus, the Jordan administration
was responsible for considerable economic progress, evidence
of which comes as a surprise to many Israelis. But along the
old borderline, the past twenty years have left their mark
like a tattoo on the landscape.

Across this dividing line, one learns something about a
former enemy as well as about oneself. Hardly another modern occupation regime has seemed on the surface so much of
a picnic, but of course this one is no picnic either. It is a
situation fraught with high drama and occasional Schweikian
comedy, human frailty, and courage. Most Israelis are still
adjusting—with difficulty, misgivings, and much confusion—
to their new and unaccustomed role as master. Few ever
anticipated this state of affairs; fewer still have been trained
in the exercise of this kind of power. So far, the situation has
been handled with humaneness and an impressive administrative talent that was rarely evinced in the past within the
borders of Israel proper. It is still marked by an atmosphere
made up of a curious—though under the circumstances entirely natural—mixture of extreme nonchalance and touchi-
ness, bad conscience and a sense of superiority, self-confidence
and fear, braggadocio and humility, sympathy and scorn,
hatred and pity. There are some who almost seem to be
saying, "Forgive us for winning," and who frantically over-
pay shopkeepers, waiters, and taxi drivers in an apparent
attempt to appease. Others have been known to loot, and to
excuse themselves with the remark, "But we shed blood
here!"—a comment which prompted one Israeli columnist to
quote Samuel Johnson: "Patriotism is the last refuge of the
scoundrel."

The Israeli as Conqueror

Some Israelis are angry at the absence of a more active spirit of cooperation on the part of the vanquished toward the victors; others despise the Arabs for sheepishly collaborating with the occupation forces. Not infrequently, both attitudes find lodgment within the same person. Some are surprised at what they see across the border, others disappointed. Oldtimers with nostalgic memories of the early forties, the last time when Palestine was a single country at peace, cross the green line only to smell jasmine, rare herbs, and deliciously charcoaled lamb. Newer immigrants and youngsters see only the dirt and the flies, the barefoot, undernourished kids in the street; they turn up their noses: "There seems to be something wrong here with the sewer." (An epidemic of stomach disorders swept Israel last summer and fall as a result of culinary expeditions into the West Bank and the Gaza Strip.) The youngsters especially, born and reared after the establishment of the state in 1948, and fully accustomed to Israel as it was before last June, are torn and do not easily know what to think. For years these lands were "abroad"—indeed not only abroad, but enemy territory. Now the children are being told by an impressive array of poets, teachers, and even some politicians that this is *moledet,* the homeland, the Jews' historic cradle, united at last with what they knew as Israel.

A few impressions of Isrealis in their new role:

The "mishpocheh" [family group]. The Israeli as conqueror is rarely alone. He travels in a company which is usually large. Everywhere in the new territory, in Sinai as on the West Bank, one notices entire families posing for photographs on burned-out or blown-up Egyptian or Jordanian tanks, like so many St. George's on their dragons. A small pickup truck, driven by a Haifa grocer, the rear overloaded with children and uncomfortable grandparents, rolls into the off-limits headquarters of the Nablus military governor, ignoring a shouting, gesticulating young guard at the gate. A heavy woman climbs out and addresses the quickly summoned officer (who is young enough to be her son) in Hungarian-accented Hebrew: *"Shalom, habbi, banu l'vaker!"* (*Shalom,* dearie, we've come to visit!)

A nonchalance and self-assurance among the military. The Israeli army of occupation, or at least that part of it in uniform, is rarely arrogant or haughty. On the contrary, the impression one gathers of the army in Gaza, Nablus, or Ramallah is one of ease, even bordering on apathy. Relaxed, calm, no doubt also bored, the typical Israeli sentry, as he mans a roadblock or guards the entry to a military installation, is usually to be seen perched on a straw armchair, feet nearly horizontal, cap tilted back, his young mouth munching away on a sweet.

At times this nonchalance can seem slightly ludicrous. In Nablus recently, I saw the military commander of the area lunching with two other senior army officers in Jacob's Well, a leading Nablus restaurant which faces the traditional site of Jesus's encounter with the Samaritan woman. The three officers were enjoying ample portions of hoummous [an Arab dish prepared with chick peas], shishkebab, and eggplant salad; one was casually leafing through a newspaper as he ate. A large radio, prominently displayed on the bar counter, was tuned to a noisy broadcast from Amman which featured a live report of King Hussein's triumphal return to his capital following a state visit to Turkey. Then the King himself spoke, promising the cheering crowd a speedy liberation from the Israeli forces oppressing their brethren on the West Bank. The officers—all of whom spoke Arabic fluently—ordered another round of beers. When the bill came, they paid and walked out, leaving a sizable tip behind. . . .

Invisible power. "One hardly sees them nowadays," says a young doctor in Ramallah. "In the beginning they were everywhere, patrolling the streets, searching houses. But not any more. I don't know why."

The massive assault of Israeli tourists has caused some residents of the West Bank to comment that there must be at least 10 million Israelis, the official figure of 2.5 million being a case of typical Jewish deception. But just as obvious as the influx of tourists is the absence of a noticeable military presence. One of the most striking characteristics of this occupation regime is its extreme thriftiness in the display of force. The overpopulated Gaza Strip, with its horrible refugee camps and slum conglomerations, is a special case in this regard, but in the hill towns and villages of the West Bank one can at times travel for days without meeting a single Israeli soldier, except for those sitting on leave at Arab cafés or hitchhiking along the road. Some villages that were searched for arms a few days after the occupation began have not seen an Israeli on duty since that time. In other places, an Israeli machine gun is to be seen about once a month. In Jericho and Nablus (the latter a hotbed of civil disobedience), a few canvas-covered tanks are parked in the courtyard of the massive police fortresses that were built by the British in the thirties and have been used since then by three occupation regimes (British, Jordanian-Bedouin, now Israeli). There are few serious shows of force, except after a particular act of terrorism or before an announced demonstration of protest. But even directly following a sniping attack on passing automobiles, or the discovery of a mined road, violent intervention remains highly selective. After some forty Al Fatah terrorists were discovered in caves and isolated plantations in Samaria, the army staged a large-scale hunt for similar bands hiding out further south in the Judean Hills—the same area where a few years earlier the famous Dead Sea scrolls had been found. A touring staff officer requested from the local commander an intelligence briefing on the area, and was told: "We have a list here of people known to be hiding weapons in their homes." His reply was: "Never mind weapons. We do not care about people hoarding machine-guns and the like. Let them live in peace. Arms as such don't interest us. We are interested only in active marauders."

A gentleness in manners. Another marked characteristic of this occupation regime remains the relative lack of military swagger, and absence of an attitude of condescension toward the masses of the vanquished, their leaders and their dignitaries. Israeli soldiers do not kick open shop doors with their boots. For goods received, all pay the full price. During the war itself, there was only one known case—subsequently severely punished—of rape. Now, nine months later, there is still no evidence of bad blood caused by soldiers "stealing" local girls. There is no black market of note; cigarettes are worth no more than their legal price of 97 agorot (28 cents). Occasionally a house is blown up in which arms have been discovered, but even this is a practice resorted to with diminishing frequency; generally, there has been an almost total absence . . . of the "mystique of destructiveness." Very rarely indeed does one hear of a soldier humiliating an Arab. Even he who may speak privately of *Arabushim* (a derogatory slang word) will in most cases behave in a polite, matter-of-fact way when encountering an Arab.

Today's Soldier, Tomorrow's Civilian

The same unfortunately cannot be said of many civilians who come into daily contact with the other side, whether as tourists, businessmen, or even as government officials on "inspection trips." It is true that the Israeli army is a people's army. Most of its personnel is nonprofessional, on reserve duty or in national service. Today's soldier is tomorrow's visiting civilian, and vice versa. Nevertheless, civilian behavior has by and large been much less understanding than that of army personnel, and has frequently given cause for bad feeling. It is invariably civilians, not soldiers, who drive through occupied cities singing patriotic tunes, or stroll the streets ostentatiously waving Israeli flags. Each city's own Arab police force, quickly reinstated and even rearmed by General Dayan soon after the conquest (much to the consternation of traditionalists and security experts) is now in charge of local law and order. Understandably, these blue-uniformed officials (the Jordanian royal crown or Egyptian half-moon carefully removed from their caps) still lack an adequate amount of self-assurance and authority. Military drivers are careful to obey their instructions, but some civilian drivers tend to ignore them or even treat them insolently. In Gaza recently, I watched two young Israelis buying corn from a street vendor. When it was time to pay, they handed him ten agorot. The vendor asked again for the regular price, some ten times higher. The boys laughed and walked on. "You lost the war," one of them called out. A few feet away stood an impassive local policeman. "Had he been asked to intervene—and that rarely happens—he would not have known what to do," an Israeli officer, in charge of the Gaza police, later remarked. . . .

Nearly everywhere on the West Bank and in the Gaza Strip, old British police fortresses are currently being repainted and refurbished. Having served Jordanian and Egyptian authorities for the past twenty years, they are now being redecorated for their newest occupants. Corridors are cluttered with timber, sacks of cement, rolls of telephone wire, and buckets of paint; Arab masons move walls, carpenters saw away at closets and doors. Within, against a background of hammering and the screeching of wooden boards, officers and civilian employees of the military government sit behind heavy Jordanian and Egyptian desks, inlaid with mother-of-pearl; the walls are hung casually with flags, army insignia, and portraits of Eshkol, Dayan, Shazar, and Rabin [Israeli leaders]. Young secretaries, girls performing their tour of duty in the national service, keep their bosses well-supplied with cups of freshly boiled tea and instant coffee.

While the occupying army takes on the settled appearance of having come to stay, the over-all number of officers in the occupation regime is still extremely limited. The first principle of the regime, as enunciated by General Dayan a few days after the war and subsequently approved by the cabinet, has been the avoidance of unnecessary friction between occupier and occupied, and maximum noninterference in local affairs. Local administration has been left almost entirely in the hands of former (elected or appointed) mayors, all of whom have remained and none of whom has yet resigned his office. Similarly, most other departments of the government—health, education, public works, social welfare, etc.—are still being managed by their previous directors, former Egyptian or Royal Jordanian civil servants. In the few cases where officials have left, their jobs have been taken over by their former deputies. A few Israeli liaison officers—in the fashion of the indirect rule of the old British colonial system—act as overseers and final arbiters of local administration. Theirs is a behind-the-scenes function; they rarely meet field personnel, and they deal mostly, and even then not very frequently, with top-level Arab officials only. Thus, health services in the occupied areas are run by seven Israelis together with 2,900 Arabs, education by nine Israelis and 4,600 Arabs, agriculture by five Israelis and 1,300 Arabs. A similar proportion is maintained in other fields of government activity, such as commerce, public works, and social welfare.

Another basic and general principle has been that 1967 will not become another 1956, when Israel was forced to withdraw from occupied Sinai after three or four months. There is a certitude that this time the occupation will last much longer, that perhaps it will last a very long time indeed, and it is best that local Arabs realize it. This does not mean that Israel will annex the occupied territories. But the assumption is that Israel is determined to hold and run these territories, with or without the cooperation of their inhabitants, until such time as there will be a permanent settlement with the Arab states. In stressing this intention, the hope of course is to encourage people to cooperate with Israel without the fear that within a few months they will be returned to Egypt and Jordan to suffer the consequences of the charge of collaboration. Such fear has been common primarily in Gaza, where residents who cooperated with Israel in 1956 were later severely dealt with by the returning Egyptians.

Success on this score has been only partial. Even in Hebron, where cooperation seems to have been greatest (to the point where Jordan has officially branded the mayor a "traitor"), most citizens still hold on to the prospect of change with the next "decisive" moment, after which Israel will surely withdraw and, if not, "we will think about it again." Such moments have been "at the end of the United Nations debates," "after the visit of . . . Mr. Jarring," "after the Khartoum summit meeting," or "after Rabat," or "as a result of King Hussein's visits, first to Cairo, then to Moscow and Washington." Such decisive moments have come and gone, followed neither by withdrawal nor by any firm commitment on the part of local Arabs; new dates will undoubtedly crop up in the future, and will continue to provide occasion for an indefinite postponement of decisions.

The principle of avoidance of unnecessary friction has forced the authorities to distinguish between vital needs and those merely desirable. The absolutely vital minimum need, as against the desirable maximum, has been to maintain the Israeli military presence and prevent terrorism. So far this has not been too difficult to achieve; terrorist activity, which at first posed a considerable menace in the new territories, has apparently been well curtailed.

Points of Friction

Aside from the prevention of terrorism, all other matters, despite the possible desirability of having it otherwise, have been left in the hands of the conquered Arabs. General Dayan stated his policy immediately after the war, in his many talks with Arab dignitaries: it was entirely up to them to lead the kind of lives they wished. If they wanted their children to go to school, if they wanted industrial and agricultural development, if they wanted to export and import, to take out loans, to produce and work, or to travel freely back and forth between the West Bank and the Arab countries for trade or pleasure, then the occupation regime would help them. If not, Israel could not care less, at least for the present. Dayan's stated policy has been widely heralded in Israel and abroad. One leading columnist went so far as to suggest that had some of the former colonial powers practiced such a policy, the course of history might have been different. No few Israelis hope that perhaps Israel will indeed succeed where others, greater and more powerful, have failed. Should a Palestinian-Arab leadership emerge that will be prepared to make a separate peace with Israel (a distinct possibility considering the utter weariness and dejection of the Palestinian Arabs after fifty years of futile conflict with the Jews and twenty years of unpopular, at times savagely repressive, Jordanian rule), many people will take it as a vindication of General Dayan's policies.

In the occupied territories themselves, things are often less clear and infinitely more complicated than might appear from a reading of neat policy papers. While the declared policy is that Israel will avoid all unnecessary points of friction, there has, for instance, been what some might term unnecessary friction in the field of education, and in such service areas as the production of electricity.

The schooling problem arose when the government last summer tried to eliminate from the Arab schools those textbooks which contained rabid anti-Israel propaganda and incitement to war. This, by itself, would have been easy; yet the government went much further. In the apparent hope of converting West Bank children to Zionism, the education ministry—which had been charged by the occupation regime with opening the Arab schools—tried to impose Israeli textbooks, complete with Arabic translations of Sholem Aleichem, Mendele Mocher Seforim, Herzl, and others, on Arab schoolchildren. Tens of thousands of textbooks had already been printed when the scandal broke. Even those Arab dignitaries who were ready and willing to cooperate with Israel, such as Mayor Joabri of Hebron who has all but burned his last bridge to Amman, considered the books not only a violation of international law but an unacceptable affront to their national dignity. The West Bank public was quick to accept rumors fed by Radio Amman that Israel wished to stamp out Muslim religious education; as a result, within days a near-total parent-teacher strike closed down all West Bank schools. Ministry officials then proposed a compromise solution: the Israeli textbooks would be withdrawn, in exchange for the censoring and, if necessary, the elimination of any offensive Arab books. This, too, might have worked; but the first step in the compromise solution was the complete cancellation of some seventy textbooks on the ground that they were dangerous as a whole. This action also met with objections, not only from Arab leaders and school officials, but from General Dayan's military governors as well, who argued that the ministry of education was being overly sensitive, was expecting the impossible, and was denying to the vanquished the last thing they had to cling to: self-dignity. Here the paradox that marks the Israelis as conquerors reemerged. The army represented in this case, as in many others, the more liberal approach, while a civilian body, in this instance, Zalman Aranne's ministry of education, took the more extreme position. . . .

A variety of reasons has been offered to explain the contradiction between policy on paper and policy in the field. One factor has been a difference of temperament among the various military leaders at different levels of command. Others which have been suggested include interdepartmental feuds, jealousy between the military and civilian establishments, and General Dayan's personal difficulties with his colleagues in Eshkol's government. But the most convincing reason that has yet been offered is also the simplest: lack of experience. As one harassed official commented recently, "Look here, *my* father had no experience in running occupied territories. Did yours?" Optimists have been encouraged by the fact that in . . . major cases of friction . . . the government finally backed down and gave in to the vanquished on practically all important points. General Dayan has always been known for his undoctrinaire approach as well as for his flexibility (a trait which has led his detractors to accuse him of a daily change of mind) . But observers here cannot remember when they have seen a government agency move as quickly under stress as Dayan's ministry of defense, which seems to be learning from past mistakes and is unhampered by considerations of personal prestige. . . .

In Israel meanwhile, the unexpected seizure of the "whole of Palestine," as well as of sizable chunks of Syria and Egypt, has given rise to a national debate of an intensity that has not been seen here since the earlier, more fervent days of Zionist colonization. An impressive number of writers, poets, and others has joined in the "Movement for the Whole of Eretz [land of] Israel." The central precept of this movement is that all of Palestine, indivisible, is part of Israel's historic birthright and must be immediately annexed—together with the Syrian Heights and Sinai. War—or, perhaps, victory—makes strange bedfellows. . . . The issue is far from exhausted. It has been suggested that the fact that none of the poets, novelists, or intellectuals who belong to the "Movement for the Whole of Eretz Israel" is younger than forty may not be sheer coincidence. Leading spokesmen on the other side are representative of a younger generation of poets and novelists. One columnist has even suggested that the "Movement for the Whole of Eretz Israel" may be a "literary and intellectual anachronism" as the "patriotic feelings" among younger people, born or reared here, are said to be "more rational, more balanced," than those of the older Zionist generation. Rather than relying on "divine promises made in the early Bronze Age," this younger generation is said to place its reliance on the "normative effect of the facts—as they presently exist—and on international law and the opinion of those who have given it recognition." But the strongest objections to annexation have come from those who, realizing there can be no large-scale immigration to Israel within the foreseeable future, fear the end of the Jewish state through the emergence of an Arab majority by 1980.

THE NEW STATUS QUO [7]

The traditional, reactionary structure of Arab society has remained unaffected by the successive political upheavals that have taken place in the Arab countries; the same Arab social class which today sends its sons to the officers' corps in Syria and Egypt did so under Farouk in Egypt and the old politicians in Syria. Algeria is an exception to this rule, both because the ruthlessness of direct French rule had the effect of pulverizing the old Arab social order and because the Algerians were after all the only Arabs who really fought for their independence and achieved it by a revolutionary struggle; hence their army represents the toughness of a revolutionary mystique and not the routine soft-job elitism of all other Arab armies. Curious as it may seem, Algeria and Israel represent the only two revolutionary societies in the Arab-Israeli orbit.

But if Arabs have historically identified with military forms of government, they have paid a stiff price through their inability to react on an adequate level to political crises and international conflicts. For the fact is that in the modern world the traditional Arab form of government is totally irrelevant. Nor can the Arab malaise be traced back to the trauma of European imperialism, on which most Arab intellectuals blame their social and political ills. In harsh truth, it was not the British and French who in most cases put an end to any purely *Arab* form of self-government in the Middle East. For at least six centuries prior to European penetration, the Arabs were ruled not by themselves but by a variety of nomadic military conquerors whose adherence to the Islamic religion made it easier to gloss over their foreignness. The Arabs were ruled by Seljuks and Ottomans, by Tartars and Mameluks; their commercial classes over the centuries consisted of Greeks, Armenians, and Jews. The basic malaise

[7] From article by Shlomo Avineri, lecturer at the Hebrew University of Jerusalem, and author of *The Social and Political Thought of Karl Marx*. *Commentary*. 45:49-53. Mr. '68. Reprinted from *Commentary*, by permission; copyright © 1968 by the American Jewish Committee.

of Arab society has been its inability to evolve an over-all social structure—the precondition of national identity. Their failure in the confrontation with Israel is thus not to be blamed merely on poor leadership or on defective policies: it is a failure that goes deep into their history. In the same way that Zionism, as a movement of national and social revolution, began with a critique not of Gentile society but of the lopsided nature of the Jewish social structure in Eastern Europe, so a parallel Arab renaissance may have to be predicated upon a prior rejection of some of the traits which have become associated with the traditional Arab consciousness. There is, however, very little evidence that such a structural rethinking is taking place among Arab intellectuals.

All this leaves Israel with a terrible dilemma. Many Israelis are experiencing severe frustration over the fact that despite the Arab military defeat the old political leaders, who were responsible for plunging the Arabs into their present catastrophe, still enjoy popularity and general esteem. That is, no rethinking of *any* kind seems to be going on in the Arab world, and the consequence may be yet another calamity when Arab leadership is again overtaken by its own rhetoric. But while everyone is now discussing the possibilities of peace, or negotiations, or nonnegotiations, in the Middle East, and in Israel hairsplitting arguments are to be heard concerning the nature of the future negotiated boundaries of Israel, it may very well turn out that future developments will not depend at all on the outcome of an agreed-upon solution. Now, after the war, everyone is a rationalist; everyone expects that the due process of international relations will bring about the preferred result of negotiated settlement. But unless something very extraordinary happens in the near future —unless, that is, the Arab governments show themselves prepared to undergo the agony of rethinking their relation to Israel—there seems little chance that any Arab government will negotiate. As for Israel, her insistence on negotiations is not a mere formalistic pedantry, but is predicated upon what seems, under the circumstances, a reasonable assumption—

that only an arrangement publicly acknowledged by the Arabs will be worth more than the paper on which it is written.

But if this is the case, and if the chances for negotiations are slim, Israel will be faced with the task of settling the future of the newly acquired territories by herself; and this is a responsibility for which she may not be as fully prepared as she was for war. It may be, in other words, that the future boundaries of the Middle East will be determined not by any conscious decision, but rather will develop as a consequence of drift, of *force des choses,* in a manner similar to the post-1945 partition of Germany, which did not come about as the consequence of an intended policy but which was a necessity imposed on all concerned by a common inability to achieve a negotiated settlement. One does not have to be excessively cynical to remark that the unnatural status quo in Germany has proved to be more durable than all the Wilsonian rhetoric of the Versailles Treaty. Similarly, in the absence of a formal peace treaty, the present cease-fire lines in the Middle East may—frightening as it may sound even to most Israelis —solidify into semipermanent borders. In that eventuality, political philosophers would be hard pressed to differentiate between the legitimacy of such boundaries and that of the old 1949 armistice lines, which became solidified in precisely the same way and remained so for nineteen years. In the absence of a negotiated settlement, the status quo becomes the only tangible reality imposed on victors and vanquished alike, sometimes to their mutual detriment. . . .

What, then, of the future? Israel has to guard against a position of romantic chauvinism (a position, incidentally, which was recently repudiated by a most impressive statement signed by outstanding figures in the academic community here). What is more important, Israel has to face a reality which is so incongruous as to require completely new political and social vistas. It is not generosity that Israel needs, but a combination of hardheaded realism with a tolerance for different customs and cultures, political astuteness coupled with a readiness on the part of Israelis—as much as on the part of the Arabs—to do away with some of the sacred cows of the immediate past: a recognition that not all the idiosyncrasies of the last nineteen years are to be taken as universal criteria or eternal verities. All this will be tough going, on both sides, but there is nothing in Zionist ideology —or in Arab history—to prevent the emergence of a solution within the new realities. It will soon be a year since the war, yet few have recognized how fundamentally the Middle East has changed. All of us go on looking for solutions, hoping for negotiations to begin, for a rational pattern to emerge, openly arrived at by reasonable and soft-spoken diplomats. Few seem to realize that the new reality is already being formed by day-to-day decisions. Awakening from the euphoria of victory and the humiliation of defeat will be a slow and painful process, for the Israelis no less than for the Arabs. Yet the process has already begun, and its development must be closely watched.

IN VICTORY THERE IS NO PEACE [8]

Opposite the Egyptian town of Ismailia, facing its cool palm groves, a handful of Israeli soldiers squat on the sandy ground. They are watching an army entertainment troupe which acts out the usual routine of skits and songs on an improvised stage. Behind the troupe rises a mound which hides the bunker built by the soldiers from Soviet materials found in the area. On the opposite bank of the Suez Canal, some two hundred yards away, a few Egyptian soldiers peer out from their trenches, eager to catch the sight and sound of the Israeli entertainers. From afar, the muffled sound of guns and mortars accompanies the troupe with sporadic thuds: the Egyptian artillery, massed along the canal, is training hard.

[8] From "A Year After the Six-Day War, Israel Still Finds That in Victory There Is No Peace," by Amnon Rubinstein, Israeli journalist and lecturer. New York *Times Magazine*. p 32-4+. Je. 2, '68. © 1968 by The New York Times Company. Reprinted by permission.

The canal, a narrow strip of water separating the enemies, is usually quiet. On the Israeli side, there is something like a holiday atmosphere: soldiers basking in the sun, lazily fishing in the greenish water, playing long games of chess on the bank, their automatic rifles close by. Tourists come to see the sights and get photographed on the very end of the local pier, Ismailia forming the background to their smiles. Plenty of time to read books, listen to the soft music and fervent harangues emanating from Radio Cairo and, perhaps, reminisce about that distant June, a year ago, when the Canal Zone was a major Egyptian military base.

Another narrow strip of water constitutes Israel's new border on the east: the River Jordan. Unlike the Suez Canal, the River Jordan is spanned by two bridges—Allenby and Damiya. At Damiya, one can see, beside the present bridge, the remains of two others. The first was blown up during the British mandate by the Jewish underground, and the second was bombed in the Six-Day War. The third is a simple affair, a Bailey bridge built by the Jordanians after the war. Its wooden planks carry a heavy traffic: trucks transporting farm produce from the West Bank of the river to Jordan, Saudi Arabia and Kuwait; buses bringing Arabs back to Israel from a visit to Mecca; cars bulging with well-to-do families on their way to see relatives in Amman.

At the improvised check post, not far from the bridge itself, a line of vehicles awaits the slow and thorough customs inspection, which is mainly a search for hidden arms and munitions. In the meantime, the passengers are going through passport control in a shabby hut. Excited children, in their Sunday clothes, run to and fro to the consternation of their parents, whose hands are full of presents purchased in Jordan —mainly huge bundles of Kleenex, which is particularly expensive in Israel. A young Arab, wearing long hair and a modish blazer, explains to a family of fellahin the intricacies of the place and directs them to the customs hut. A harassed Israeli official tries to introduce some order by shouting the few Arabic words he has recently learned.

A distinguished-looking Arab lady, sitting in her husband's Mercedes, is being interviewed by a foreign journalist:

"Madam, where are you going?"

"To Amman, to visit my sister and my family. I have not seen them since the war."

"Will you come back?"

"Come back? Naturally; this is my home, my country."

"But do you want to return and live under the Israelis?"

"With the grace of Allah, there will be peace. One day."

"But until then .... How is life under Israeli rule?"

"All the Israelis I met were very nice people and, with the grace of Allah ...."

"May I quote you? May I have your name ... ?"

"No, no. Please, no. I am not a political person. I know not. No names, please."

During the past year, Damiya has not always been like this. A short distance from the customs hut, several craters, hardly noticeable, are the sole reminder of the blood shed here periodically. At Damiya, war and peace alternate madly. Last March, one day after Israeli troops moved across the bridge on a raid into Jordan, normal traffic—commerce, tourists, family reunions—was resumed. And, often, traffic at Damiya, continues while only a few miles away—to the north or south—guns are exchanging fire.

The Tel Aviv University auditorium—white and sterile under fluorescent lights—is packed with students listening to a public debate. One of their faculty, Uri Rapp, is speaking with mounting excitement in favor of a Palestinian federation uniting Israel with Falastin, as the Arab part of Palestine is sometimes called.

"This country is the legitimate homeland of two nations," he exclaims to the sound of scattered applause. "It is a conflict between two justices: our justice and their justice. The only solution is a compromise: two states linked together by a federation."

"Why don't you go and convince the Arabs first?" shouts one student.

"First of all, we have got to know what we want to do."

The next speaker, a fiery nationalist, preaches for immediate annexation of the occupied territories: "This is our land, our country. All of it! He who questions our right to the mountains of Judea must also question our right to Tel Aviv."

From the back rows someone intervenes: "And what about the Arabs? What about more than a million people who were born here? What will you do with them?"

Fruits of Victory

These snapshots are characteristic of postwar Israel. The public mood has altered in the course of the past year. A year ago all Israelis shared one dominant mood—whether anxiety in May, or elation after the June victory. The issue then was simple and clear, as simple and clear as the difference between life and death.

Victory brought with it a new sense of strength, but also a host of new, intricate problems which have plunged the country into oceans of debate. It goes on everywhere: in the Knesset [parliament], in public forums like the one at Tel Aviv University, in the press, in cafés, in living rooms. Citizens' committees have sprung up and flood the newspapers with advertisements exhorting the public, denouncing the government for its alleged defeatism (or, alternatively, its militancy), soliciting recruits, publishing petitions of intellectuals, poets and painters supporting their cause.

But the diversity is not only in matters of opinion. The feelings, too, are mixed: self-confidence coupled with a sober resignation; a new sense of Israel's vitality plus a certain feeling of frustration; some hope, some bewilderment.

The self-confidence, the exhilaration, can be seen in the assurance with which Israelis stroll along the Suez Canal, within sight of thousands of Egyptian soldiers, within range of hundreds of Soviet-built guns and tanks. Israeli tourists still storm the new territories by the thousands, reaching into remote Arab villages, climbing the mountains of Samaria, descending into the Jordan Valley, unarmed and unharmed.

Their eagerness to see every inch of the new territories is incredible. In the one postwar year, more than 40,000 have visited the remote monastery of St. Catherine's in the heart of the Sinai, a seven-hour ride through trackless desert from the nearest surfaced road. (This flood forced the astounded Greek Orthodox monks to impose visiting hours, for the first time in the monastery's quiet history, and to provide a Hebrew-speaking monk as full-time tourist guide; solitude is the last thing they will have for a long time to come.)

Says a young law student in Tel Aviv: "I couldn't care less what the final settlement is, as long as I can get onto my scooter and drive up to Nablus." Many of the popular songs express this thirst for space. "When Peace Comes," oddly one of the war's popular songs, runs:

> When peace comes, when peace comes,
> Egyptian football teams will beat us in Tel Aviv,
> We shall go by train to Damascus,
> We shall go skiing to the Lebanon.

The postwar year has not seen peace, but last winter Israelis did ski on the snowy slopes of the Golan Heights, while others bathed in the sunny waters of the Tiran Strait.

This craving for travel may be discounted by outsiders as a marginal factor in the over-all issues facing Israel. In reality, this need for breathing space is of major importance to Israelis. Only those who have lived for twenty years sealed within a state the size of New Jersey can appreciate the power behind this need, not for domination, but for freedom of movement. A return to prewar Israel would be a return to claustrophobia—more suffocating than before, after the taste of spaciousness.

This feeling of space is merely one attribute of a new sense of power. The war demonstrated Israel's inherent vitality—this after a prolonged internal crisis and years of political malaise. But the war did something more: It shattered the long-cherished dream of "instant peace" which would come in the wake of the ultimate total victory.

For twenty years many Israelis harbored this wishful dream, that the Arabs, once realizing the futility of their effort to destroy Israel, would come to terms with her. On the eve of the war, many Israelis believed it was going to be a case of "either/or." Says a young kibbutznik [member of an agricultural commune], in a book of recorded interviews with soldiers who fought in the war: "When the war started, I said to myself: 'Anyway, this is going to be the last war. If we defeat the Arabs this time, this will be the end to fighting and then there will be peace.'" He, like many Israelis, was to be disappointed. He failed to take account of the irrational, all-engulfing Arab hatred of Israel. Israelis did not—perhaps could not—recognize the deep roots of suspicion, nourished by propaganda, out of which grew this hate.

The decisive victory has not produced any real change of Arab heart. There are, it is true, some signs of a new realism in the Arab world but these are insignificant. The over-all picture has not changed, and common sense still withers under the Middle Eastern sun.

Thus, the war has shattered two illusions: on the Arab side, the illusion of their ability to destroy Israel; on the Israeli side, that of a quick reconciliation with the Arabs. The Arabs will have to give up their impossible, bloody dream of annihilating the Jews and will have to live with a new Israel—strong, secure, sure of itself. The Israelis, on the other hand, will have to learn the art of living in an indefinite state of nonpeace.

The idea is not very pleasant but it will not be an entirely new art. For twenty years Israel has lived in a state of *de facto* war. This war has had its fluctuations according to the political circumstances prevailing in the Middle East. It has alternated between overt military acts, sabotage and guerrilla warfare, and has always been accompanied by open belligerence and economic boycott. This constant war has not ceased

in the last year, but Israel's new position of strength renders
her much less vulnerable to its effects.

Paradox of Cooperation

If the prospects of a quick peace have faded during the
postwar year, a new *modus vivendi* has been established between the belligerents. The Six-Day War has paradoxically
brought about more cooperation between Arab and Jew than
the eighteen preceding years of armistice agreements. This
cooperation has two channels—the link across the Jordan
River and the daily experience of coexistence on the West
Bank.

The Damiya Bridge illustrates this new *modus vivendi*.
For the first time, there is an ordinary border station along
Israel's boundary, through which people commute between
Israel and an Arab country. For the first time, there is economic interchange and the benefits of trade and cooperation
are not merely an abstract idea but are expressed in hard
cash. The bridge is the outcome of facts of life defying politics, of the victory of common sense over prejudice. True, it
is a temporary bridge, but many hope that it will be a permanent bridge, in more than the literal sense, between Arab
and Jew.

The Israeli occupation of the West Bank is a new experience. Its central concept was formulated by Moshe Dayan,
the minister of defense, whose postwar record shines as
brightly as his military career. It is as simple as it is ingen-
ious. Says Colonel Shlomo Gazit, administrative head of the
new territories:

Our principle is not to intervene in the affairs of the inhabitants.
This means that they continue to have recourse to their own organizations and officials. If they want our assistance, we are ready
to help. Otherwise, we are interested only in security matters.

The nonintervention policy has some extreme manifesta-
tions: The school system is now independent and is run by
a West Bank Educational Council. Arab nationalist literature
is sold freely; an ex-Jordanian Minister, Anwar Nuseibeh,

states at a public gathering in Tel Aviv that the war was an
Israeli act of aggression; the Israeli radio broadcasts in a
direct transmission from El Aksa Mosque in Jerusalem the
Friday Muslim sermons without prior checking, although
these sermons are frankly of a political and nationalistic
nature. When two Arab judges refused to allow Israeli lawyers to plead before them—contrary to an order issued by the
military command—they were neither dismissed nor repri-
manded; rather, the military command announced that it
would reconsider the validity of its order in the light of the
Arab judges' opinion.

The results of this unprecedented occupation can be seen
on the West Bank and in the Gaza Strip, where the great
numbers of Israeli sightseers stand in contrast to the very
few Israeli military personnel visible. The whole military
administration of the new territories—32,000 square miles
and more than a million inhabitants—numbers 249 Israelis,
while the local Arab civil service numbers 9,713 men. It is
this regime which is responsible for the relative failure of the
terror inside Israel.

In evaluating the effects of the terror during the past
year, two facts must be remembered: First, the ordinary escalation which leads from acts of sabotage through retaliation
to widespread resistance, has up to now been avoided; second,
the terror is waged not from within, but from outside, from
across the Jordan River. The terrorists cannot find shelter
among the local Palestinians. Of the 1,500 terrorists now in
Israeli prisons, many, perhaps most, were captured through
information given by Arab villagers and townsfolk. Consequently, the terrorists cannot stay in Israel for more than one
night and usually cross the river into Jordan before early
light. This limits their scope of action and explains why most
acts of sabotage occur along the frontier and not deeper inside Israel.

The attitude of the Palestinians is significant. Naturally,
there is an element of deterrence; the Arabs are afraid of
having their houses blown up by the Israeli Army as punish-

ment. But no one forces them to volunteer information. They do so because they themselves do not want the terror. They have something to lose if the situation deteriorates.

Obviously, they resent Israeli rule. Says a prominent Nablus lawyer: "The best occupation is bad enough." But life under the Israelis is bearable and one can carry on with relative dignity, certainly without humiliation.

Moreover, though some groups—like hoteliers, lawyers and travel agents—have suffered economically since the war, the Arab population on the West Bank has fared tolerably well during this last year and will probably fare better in the future. Despite the terrorists' threats, Arab fellahin visit the government agricultural shows at which Israeli instructors demonstrate the advantages of new techniques, modern tools, better seeds and varied crops. A cigarette factory in East Jerusalem has tripled its output by comparison with previous years. Public works on a large scale supply jobs for the unemployed; loans are given by the government for reconstruction and development purposes. All this is something which may be lost if terror reigns.

In the meantime, something has already been won. Direct contact has rebutted the image of the Israelis built up in the Arab mind by years of propaganda. For the young Arab, this was the first encounter with the mythical men from across the border, and instead of the alleged monstrous beast —half wolf and half mouse—they found people who, although unwanted, although alien, could be talked to and lived with.

On the Israeli side, too, something new happened. A tremendous interest in things Arabic is sweeping the country. Suddenly there is a will to learn Arabic; books, courses and self-instruction records abound. The radio has introduced a series of daily lessons in spoken Arabic. Jerusalem's Mayor Teddy Kollek has ordered all public signs and official notices to be written in both languages. Arab and Jewish soccer teams meet regularly.

For the Palestinian Arab the postwar year has also meant more space. The sea, which could be seen from the Judean hills, became accessible; thousands of Arabs flock to the Tel Aviv beach, staring with equal astonishment at the waves and the bikinis. But the disappearance of the armistice line means more than that. Arab families split in 1948 could, for the first time, reunite. Skilled labor is beginning to benefit by the much higher Israeli standard of living; the wages of Arab and Israeli workers are moving toward equalization.

Again, this does not mean that the Arabs welcome the postwar situation. But daily life can be carried on without encountering the presence of an occupying force. The Israelis —notorious for their sharp tongues and blunt frankness—have been extremely careful not to hurt Arab feelings. This record has occasionally been marred: The employment of women by the military administration is regarded by Arab males as offensive, and the military parade on Independence Day which marched through the Arab sectors of Jerusalem was a tactless and unnecessary affair.

But, on the whole, the postwar year has demonstrated the liberalism and tolerance which characterize Israel. No death sentence has been passed on Arab terrorists, including the perpetrators of the most foul and cowardly murders. A death sentence passed by an Arab court on an Arab in Gaza has been commuted to life imprisonment as a result of Israeli intervention.

There is one outstanding feature which proves that life under Israeli rule, even if unwanted, is tolerable, and that is the total failure of any attempt at civil resistance, so much urged by the Arab states. Actually, in the postwar year there have been fewer strikes—a traditional political weapon in the Middle East—than in the prewar year, when political demonstrations and strikes against King Hussein's regime were rife.

Coming to Terms

The Middle East conflict was born in Palestine and it stands to reason that it is there it should begin to die. The way out of the present deadlock may bypass Cairo and Amman. Many Israelis have arrived at the conclusion that Israel should come to terms with the Palestinians and that in this course lies some hope for stability in the region.

The Palestinian Arabs, excepting a courageous minority, have up to now refused to deal with Israel or even to establish their own leadership above the level of local authorities. The Israeli government did not object to their sending a delegation to the Arab summit conference but even that suggestion was defeated. The Mayor of Nablus, Hamdi Canaan, explained to me that such a step "would be a stab in the back of the Arab people," but then qualified this by adding, "at least as long as the Palestine problem is being dealt with in the international arena."

The Palestinians' refusal to negotiate directly with Israel is also motivated by fear of Jordanian reprisals when, and if, Israel withdraws. As time goes by, the Palestinians may despair of their protectors in Cairo and Amman, as well as of the much-awaited "miracle" coming from the "international arena." This possible change in mood, plus the realization that Israel does not want to dominate them, but is interested only in safeguarding its own security, may lead to a direct settlement between Arabs and Jews in their common land.

Admittedly, this view is merely one of many. Public opinion is split and perhaps for the first time in Israel's history the traditionally monolithic parties' barriers have broken down. The argument goes on within the parties as much as it does among them. Even the ruling Labor party has failed to formulate any sort of common policy, its leaders expressing a plethora of views, ranging from Minister of Labor Yigal Allon's semiannexationist utterances to Foreign Minister Abba Eban's opposition to any change of the status quo. The debate concerns even matters of terminology: Should the new territories be referred to as "liberated" or "occupied"? After much haggling, the government finally decided to avoid the issue by referring to them as "held territories."

One extreme opinion, held mainly by the marginal New Communist party, as well as by some prominent members of Israel's ever-active lunatic fringe, calls for immediate and unconditional withdrawal. At the other extreme is the Greater Israel Movement, which advocates immediate annexation of all the new territories. This movement—which, in keeping with Israeli tradition, split in two, the splinter faction demanding "action"—includes prominent persons from many parties and walks of life, notably the author Moshe Shamir, reserve General Avraham Joffe and publisher Oved Ben Ami. It has been very active and its public assemblies attract large crowds.

Another body, the League for an Israel-Falastin Federation, headed by Uri Avnery, a member of the Knesset and editor of the sensational weekly *Ha'olam Hazeh*, attracts many young intellectuals. It argues for the establishment of an Arab state in Palestine united with Israel by some sort of federated arrangement. It bitterly attacks the Greater Israel Movement. Annexation, the league claims, would mean either an Arab majority within the foreseeable future—there is already one Arab to every two Jews if the new territories are taken into account—or some form of political discrimination against the Arabs, something most Israelis reject instinctively.

The cabinet itself is split, but has found shelter behind the government's declared policy. This states that there will be no change in the status quo without a permanent peace settlement arrived at by direct negotiations. Eban supports this refusal to divulge Israel's plans by arguing that any unilateral concession at this stage, without reciprocal concessions on the part of the Arab states, would be foolish and bad politics. Premier Levi Eshkol makes the same point by saying that "we shall not play poker with ourselves." This attitude may be sound policy, but it is also a cover for the cabinet's failure to make up its mind how Israel should play its hand, when and if the game starts.

Members of the cabinet are usually content with expressing two negative statements with regard to a hypothetical peace settlement. First, there will be no return to the prewar borders; second, the present cease-fire lines are not necessarily the final peace boundaries. The hawks—such as Allon and Minister Without Portfolio Menahem Begin, leader of the Herut party—stress the first proposition. The doves—headed by Eban and including the two leftist Mapam ministers, Mordechai Bentov and Israel Barbilai—emphasize Israel's readiness to give up some territory in return for peace and object to the settlement of Jewish civilians on the West Bank.

True to his nature, Moshe Dayan has expressed some personal and rather unorthodox views. Immediately after the war, he advocated a deal with King Hussein, giving back to Jordan civil control over a great part of the West Bank and placing Islam's holy places in Jerusalem under Arab sovereignty. But recently he has become more and more convinced of the feasibility of a direct settlement with the Palestinians. In an interview with the newspaper *Ma'ariv*, published on the eve of Independence Day, he said:

> I now see a prospect for the Jewish people and the Palestinian Arabs to live together—and I confess that this possibility is much more concrete now than I ever previously believed. . . . When I say that the Palestinians are ready for coexistence with us, not just in words but in reality, I am not voicing a desire but am summarizing facts and talks with the Palestinians. . . .

Land in Return for Peace

Despite this divergence, the great majority of Israelis are united on one issue: support for the government's policy that without a peace treaty there should be no territorial change. This is borne out by a poll conducted last April by the Labor daily *Davar*. Of 1,200 Jewish Israelis questioned, 87 per cent objected to any territorial change without peace. Significantly, 78 per cent were ready to give back some territory in return for peace.

This may be misleading to the foreign reader. When Israelis agree to withdrawal in return for peace, they generally mean a peace with built-in guarantees more than a mere document. Israelis cherish the memory of the June victory but they remember, perhaps with deeper intensity, the May trauma. Words and documents will just no longer suffice. The idea that Arab forces should be allowed to return to the precise vantage points from which a new war could be launched is anathema to most Israelis. Demilitarization of a major part of the new territories will therefore be a required minimum.

"The present borders," says General Ariel (Arik) Sharon, "are not borders of peace. They are war-prevention borders." Few Israelis would be ready to give up this asset in return for words and papers, even if the Arabs were ready to consider such a deal.

ARAB GUERRILLAS: A WAY OF LIFE [9]

"The Arabs' only option is resistance," Dr. Mohammed H. el-Zayyat, the Egyptian government's spokesman, said to an American. "Would you deny us what you encouraged in your European allies twenty-five years ago?"

Resistance feeds the demand for revenge and, most important, offers a unifying focus for 110 million Arabs otherwise sharply divided by ideology and economic standards.

That those standards are rising as oil revenues increase and compulsory education spreads does not alter, in the view of most Arabs, the need for continuing what amounts to an old-fashioned blood feud with Israel.

Little Military Effect

At present the resistance has little military effect. But Israeli general officers, considering the available resources of the Arab world, concede that the resistance could become much more dangerous than occasional harassment.

[9] From "The Arab World: Guerrilla War a Way of Life," one of a series of articles by Drew Middleton, staff correspondent. New York *Times*. p 1. Je. 15, '68. © 1968 by The New York Times Company. Reprinted by permission.

Foreign diplomats think the resistance has political importance. An American suggested that it might even have politically constructive value if, through it, "Arab confidence is restored to the point where they will feel able to negotiate with Israel as equals."

A Briton said that "the time to take the resistance seriously is when Al Fatah starts cutting the throats of Arabs collaborating with the Jews."

Al Fatah is the most adventurous, the best armed and the most publicized of the resistance groups.

At a convention of the Palestinian National Assembly now taking place in Cairo, there have been indications of closer teamwork between Al Fatah and the more prosperous Palestine Liberation Organization. Heretofore, the organizations have been bitter rivals. . . .

The chief political reason for Arab support of Al Fatah, the Palestine Liberation Organization and other guerrilla groups is the conviction that Israel is not prepared to withdraw from the territory she occupied in Jordan, Syria and the United Arab Republic during the 1967 war. The conviction is reinforced by the belief that the United States, thought by many in the Arab world to exercise decisive influence over Israel, does not intend to force her to withdraw.

Only Course of Action

Consequently, the Arabs reason that resistance is the only means of forcing Israeli evacuation from the Sinai Peninsula, the West Bank of the Jordan River and the Golan heights of Syria.

Despite recent reports of proposed concessions by the Egyptians, the diplomatic efforts of Ambassador Gunnar V. Jarring of Sweden, named by the United Nations Security Council last November [1967] to promote a settlement, appear to have produced little of substance.

Israel seeks peace, according to a senior official in her foreign ministry, through face-to-face negotiations with the Arabs leading to a settlement that will provide maximum security with the minimum of Arabs in the country. With-drawal from the occupied territories must be part of arrange-ments for the nation's future security, the Israelis insist. Those arrangements would include mutually guaranteed Is-raeli frontiers under individual peace treaties with the Arab nations.

Privately and publicly, Arab leaders have rejected direct negotiations with the Israelis.

Hints from King Hussein of Jordan represent a faint sign of change on the Arab side. The King, his intermediaries have told Israel, might negotiate—through a third party—a peace that would recover his lost lands and allow Israel the secure frontiers she seeks.

But the King would do so only if he could be sure that President Gamal Abdel Nasser of the United Arab Republic could not arouse the Arab world, including Jordan's un-official opposition, the National Charter Group, against him. The group consists of army officers, civil servants, trade unionists and politicians who oppose any concessions to the Israelis.

In the virtually unanimous view of non-Egyptian leaders and politicians, President Nasser's stature among Arabs has been drastically reduced by last year's defeat and his country's increased dependence on Soviet aid. In the circumstances he can do little more than blame Israeli intransigence for the diplomatic stalemate and try to stimulate a disillusioned people toward greater economic and military efforts.

Syria, the third and most intransigent of the principal Arab combatants, has refused to have anything to do with Dr. Jarring's mission.

So the guerrilla effort goes on, with financial support from throughout the Arab world.

In the atmosphere of shock and shame arising from the defeat last year, Arab leaders as varied as King Hassan II of Morocco, President Abdel Rahman Arif of Iraq and Premier Abdul Hamid Bakush of Libya give public support for the resistance as the main expression of the Arab will to continue the fight.

Repeatedly the visitor is told that the "wrong" of Israel's existence, inflicted on the Arabs by the West, must be righted, certainly by Israel's withdrawal to the prewar frontiers, hopefully by her defeat and the creation of a new, Arab, Palestinian state.

"I would support a Palestinian state where Arab and Jew lived together," King Faisal of Saudi Arabia said. "But there must be no foreign Jews living there or coming there."

"We think only of revolution and victory," said Yasser Arafat who, under the name Abu Amer, is one of Al Fatah's field commanders. "We will win back our country from the Jews."

The guerrillas expect a long struggle. They do not see 1948 or 1956 or 1967—the years in which Arab armies were routed by the Israelis—as defeats, but as reverses on the way to final victory.

ISRAEL: TWENTY YEARS AFTER [10]

The stillness of a Jerusalem Sabbath was pleasantly broken . . . [last spring] when the sounds of a children's party drifted onto a street in the tree-lined Talbieh neighborhood.

Suddenly, an accordion broke into the rollicking music of "Hava Nagila," and the group began to sing the lively and familiar song, which means "Let us be joyful."

Then, changing mood abruptly, the plaintive melody of "Sharm el Sheikh," could be heard, an immensely popular song of the war last June that recalls a soldier's thoughts as he heads toward the Sinai outpost that controls the Strait of Tiran and access to Israel's southern port, Elath.

The tunes spanned Israel's twenty years, one recalling the Zionists' hope and the enthusiasm that surrounded the birth

[10] From "After 2 Decades and 3 Wars, Diverse Land of Israel Is Still Trying to Find Its Way," by James Feron, staff correspondent, New York *Times.* p 16. My. 2, '68. © 1968 by The New York Times Company. Reprinted by permission.

of Israel, the other a lingering, uncertain expression of Israel today.

Israel's two decades will be celebrated . . . [May 2, 1968] with a parade that will wind more than five miles through formerly divided Jerusalem, unified in the war last year.

The decision to flaunt Israel's military might before the Arabs, and indications that the move was not universally popular at home, are typical of modern Israel. Like any twenty-year-old, she is still trying to find her way.

That way seems to remain uncertain. Nearly one year after her third war with the Arab states surrounding her, Israel is in virtually the same position, although in control of considerably more territory, that she was in 1948.

Facing a Hostile Egypt

To the west, the United Arab Republic sits across the Suez Canal, watching Israelis in control of the east bank and the vast Sinai Peninsula behind. . . . [In April 1968] President Gamal Abdel Nasser said that another war with Israel was inevitable.

To the north, Lebanon remains the most benign of Israel's neighbors. Israelis say that they don't know who will be the first to make peace with Israel, but that Lebanon will be a quick second.

Syria, to the northeast, is so hostile that she refuses even to deal with Dr. Gunnar V. Jarring, the United Nations envoy who has been trying to bring the parties in the June war together for negotiations.

To Israelis, Jordan appears the most likely to talk peace because she lost the most in the war, because she remains, like Israel, accessible to Western influence, and because she maintains the only contact with Israel through an open border along the cease-fire line.

But the Jordanians appear to be unable to move without Cairo's assent, so Israel sits astride conquered lands, her ministers arguing over what to do about them and taking contradictory actions to solidify their positions. The prospect is for a long occupation.

Israel today is as varied as her landscape. Situated in the land of ancient Canaan, the "Promised Land" sought by Moses, she has much of what her modern founders envisaged —not all, but much. . . .

The 7,000 square miles allotted to Israel by the United Nations became 8,000 square miles when the armistice lines were drawn up after the [1948] war. The Israelis had gained the Galilee, most of which was to have been allotted to the Arabs, and a corridor leading to Jerusalem, which was to have been internationalized under the United Nations plan.

Jerusalem was a city divided between Jordan and Israel. About 600,000 Palestinian Arabs had fled from Israel, but 56,000 remained. The Jewish population numbered 716,000.

A new flow of immigration began. Jewish communities that had lived in relative tranquillity in the largely Muslim states surrounding Israel began to move out under the frictions created by the war and its aftermath.

These were Sephardic, or "Oriental," Jews from the Atlas Mountains of Morocco and Algeria, the hills of Yemen, the Jewish quarters of Cairo or the villas of Baghdad and Damascus. They changed the face of Israel.

Shoshana is tall and pretty, with dark curly hair. She came to Israel as an infant, from Iraq, with a family that was wealthy enough for her father "to go to London once a year to check on his money."

She joined a youth movement in high school and was directed, as many members were, to a kibbutz. Her decision to go shocked her family.

"They didn't understand," she said. "They're still living in Baghdad and they still see things through those eyes."

"You have a man from the Atlas Mountains with ten kids," Premier Levi Eshkol said in an interview. "Try to talk to him about a communal kitchen, much less Karl Marx or socialism."

Israel adjusted her plans. Development towns were established, like Arad in the northern Negev. School days were lengthened in immigrant areas to enable children from crowded homes to study in more accommodating circumstances. Entrance levels for high schools were lowered for the Sephardim.

Israel today has 2,344,000 Jews, of whom about half are members of the Middle Eastern immigration. The atmosphere of second-class citizenship is diminishing, but the Sephardim remain essentially outside the mainstream of political life.

Perhaps the greatest force for equality in Israel has been the military. It has become a part of the social fabric and in many ways it is the most clearly definable thread tying together all segments of Israeli life.

Colonel Mordechai Bar-On, the army's chief education officer, says:

> We have reached a situation now where the percentage from the Oriental communities is close to 50 per cent, which corresponds to their share among the population.
> When they leave the army . . . , they no longer feel isolated. They are not strangers in their own country.

The fighting force grew from the pre-1948 Haganah. The size of the standing army today is a military secret, but a good guess would put it at 60,000 or 70,000, the size of Haganah at the peak of the 1948 war.

But, by using the reserve force, the army can be expanded in a few days to a highly specialized, well-coordinated force of 300,000.

Young men serve for three years, unmarried young women twenty months. It is something of an embarrassment not to serve.

Israel's founders remain her leaders, elderly Russian-born Zionists who lead political parties that each year become less distinguishable from each other and seem to become less in touch with the masses.

"I think today's Israeli youth is convinced that the achievements in the state so far have been not in politics, but in deeds," Professor Yigal Yadin, the archeologist and former chief of staff, said.

A Dozen Parties

"Yigal Allon certainly symbolizes the younger generation for many thousands of people," he went on, referring to the forty-eight-year-old minister of labor and former commander of the Palmach, the striking arm of Haganah. "And Moshe Dayan is certainly a member of the 'generation of the state,' " he added, speaking of the fifty-three-year-old defense minister.

Voters cast a single ballot, for the party, not the man. Each party offers a list of 120 candidates for all the seats in parliament. Representation is determined by each party's share of the national vote.

This system has produced an excess of parties—a dozen at the moment, that split, merge, split and reform constantly. The merger of three into the Israel Labor party last year may enable the party to gain a majority, the first in Israel's voting history, in the November 1969 general elections.

A majority would eliminate what has always been a crucial necessity for seeking coalition partners and it could diminish the influence of pivotal religious parties.

Religion has been a cause of many divisions in Israel. Sabbath laws are imposed on observant and nonobservant alike. Except where opposition can make itself felt.

Municipal buses do not run on the Sabbath in Jerusalem, except in the annexed Arab sector. They do run in Haifa, a workers' city where the power of the labor union is supreme. No Jew can obtain a civil marriage in Israel and the Reform and Conservative branches of Judaism remain unrecognized.

There is a different feeling about religion among many young people in Israel—a search for associations with their past. "The religion of history," Professor Yadin calls it.

The Sabra, or native Israeli, has become something of a stranger to those who came here decades ago. He is tough, impatient, unsophisticated and unapologetic. He has no inferiority complex about being a Jew. The opposite is more the case.

He has never experienced anti-Semitism and might describe it, as a fourteen-year-old psychiatrist's son did recently, as hating Jews "more than is necessary."

In the last twenty years, 100,000 to 150,000 Jews have left Israel, some after being here only a short time. One of Israel's major interests these days is in trying to lure back the young men and women, especially those who left to seek opportunity elsewhere.

One way is with highly technical industry. Planners are beginning to dismantle some of the cumbersome and outmoded state-constructed apparatus, bureaucratic as well as industrial, to replace it with export earners that might better utilize the nation's size, manpower and resources.

A Vibrant Economy

The economy has expanded rapidly, spurred by immigration and helped by the Jews of the world. The gross national product has grown from $240 million in 1952—at current prices—to $3.43 billion last year.

It has grown at a rate of 10 per cent a year for most of the last decade. Now, the Israeli worker enjoys a per capita income of about $1,000 a year, about the level of Italian, Dutch and Austrian workers.

Over the years, Israel has enjoyed the financial assistance of donations, reparations, restitution, loans and other outside help. Yitzhak Taub, assistant to the governor general of the Bank of Israel, estimates that this type of assistance constitutes 9 to 10 per cent of the total resources available to Israel.

Dr. Israel Goldstein, president of Keren Hayesod, a worldwide fund-raising arm of the Jewish Agency, says that Jews of the world have contributed $1.5 billion to Israel over twenty years, three quarters of it from the United States.

A total of $864 million in World War II reparations was paid to Israel over more than a decade by West Germany. Although this income has ended, considerable sums of foreign currency accumulate in Israel through German restitution payments to individuals who suffered under the Nazi regime.

Israel's balance of trade has produced huge deficits over the years, climbing steadily to $477 million in 1966.

Severe government controls were imposed, lowering the deficit to $212 million last year, but growth came to a virtual halt and unemployment soared.

Israel's major export earners are citrus fruit, polished diamonds and tourism. The state has virtually no natural resources. Water brought from the Sea of Galilee to the northern Negev has helped increase the amount of irrigated land from 75,000 acres in 1948 to 712,000 today.

Some would like to see Israel become the hothouse of Europe. Others see it as the Switzerland of the Middle East.

The undoubted prosperity that has accrued to the Jews of Israel has also accrued to the Arabs of Israel, making them, the Israelis say proudly, the most prosperous Arabs in the Middle East. But these 300,000 Arabs find it difficult to get work in Jewish business and remain socially unintegrated.

Most Israeli Arabs are not permitted to fight for their country. They understand the reasons for barring them from combat with Arabs who may literally be their cousins.

It is not likely that the Arabs who left in 1948 will ever return. If there is a solution to the refugee problem, it will not be through resettlement in Israel. The nation's leaders have enough to worry about in the decline in Jewish immigration.

Few Jews are coming now. Gila, an eighteen-year-old at Hebrew University, may have been one of the last to arrive from the Soviet Union, where the three-million-member Jewish community represents Israel's large hope of large-scale immigration.

Gila's family left the Soviet Union June 4, the day before the war that brought a break in Israeli-Soviet relations and an end to the trickle of Jewish emigration.

As far as Gila is concerned, she is in the West. "I can go to the beach, buy pretty clothes, do anything," she says.

In Tel Aviv, a secretary can earn about 550 Israeli pounds, about $157 a month. A beginning faculty member at a university gets a bit less than twice that.

Installing a telephone costs $130. A $100 tax is imposed on foreign travel. A new television set costs about $400.

Services are somewhat cheaper than in the United States, but many food prices are higher. A cleaned, packaged chicken in a supermarket is sold for about 70 cents a pound, more than twice the American price. American diplomats get a slight cost-of-living allowance. Many Israeli wives work.

Most Israelis purchase their apartments. An apartment with more than two bedrooms is unusual, no matter how big the family. The apartments have balconies and plants, often with vines crawling throughout the rooms. Danish-modern furniture is the big thing, but it is expensive. The walls will be covered with modern art or maps, the shelves filled with archeological souvenirs or reminders of the occupant's land of origin.

What is the outlook? Israelis like to think in terms of peace, but the outlook for peace is dismal. The political outlook is for change, the replacement of the men who came in the early years of the century with men who were born in this era, and this area.

Jews will always come to taste the life here, and some will stay, but not by the tens of thousands. The local Arab population will continue to outpace the Jewish population, and this may change Israel further. The country will become more a part of its region.

The economy will become more specialized, leaning toward export markets, but it may never become entirely self-sufficient.

Although the religious squabbles will go on forever Israelis have become comfortable with their day-to-day religion. There is less synagogue attendance here than in many Jewish communities abroad, but there is no concern over what to do about Jewish holidays because they are national holidays in Israel.

The young Israeli will probably continue to turn inward, a victim of the siege mentality. But he remains full of enthusiasm and does not believe, as his parents did, that there is any question of Israel's survival. His state is the product of twenty years of challenge. He does not care what it might have been, had there been peace. He only knows that he will have to fight for it again.

IV. THE WAR AND THE WEST

EDITOR'S INTRODUCTION

The three Western powers—the United States, France, and Great Britain—found themselves in a quandary, when, contrary to expectations, Israel invaded Egypt, Syria, and Jordan. Both London and Washington took equivocal positions, refusing outright condemnation of the Israeli attack while withholding support from the Arab states. While the posture of neutrality may have been politically expedient, it gained no friends in the Middle East. Israel felt let down, if not betrayed, by the Western powers; the Arabs accused Britain and the United States of collusion with Israel, and when this argument was shown to be patently false, still asserted that the Americans and the British were definitely in sympathy with the Israelis.

Only General de Gaulle characteristically took a forthright stand, one which shocked French public opinion and appalled Israel. He announced that France remained neutral but also made it clear that Israel was in the wrong; by so doing, he openly wooed the Arab states. Moreover, the Israelis, dependent on French military hardware and, as the *New Yorker's* correspondent Genêt stresses, enjoying what they believed to be "an informal, friendly alliance" with France, saw themselves as finally cut off from any meaningful support from the Western powers. Israel, if she did not know it before, knew now that she would have to "go it alone" in any military engagement with the Arabs.

De Gaulle's policy was calculated to make France the dominant Western influence among the Arabs, replacing Britain and the United States in this regard. France has declared that she will sell her arms to the Arabs, and in light of the effective use made of French armaments by the Israelis, there seems little doubt that the Arabs will buy. France, General de Gaulle apparently believes, according to Henry Tanner in the New York *Times*, must try to counter Soviet power and influence in the area. But the limitations of French economic power are such that France, though she may play a leading Western role among the Arab nations in the near future, will hardly prove a counterweight to Russia.

Perhaps in recognition of the imbalance of power that will exist in the Middle East while the U.S.S.R. and France supply arms to the Arabs, the United States finally decided in October 1968 to negotiate with Tel Aviv on the sale of supersonic jet fighter-bombers. Washington and Moscow, by exporting armaments, may end up by fighting each other by proxy.

LETTER FROM PARIS [1]

Because General de Gaulle founded his career and the salvation of contemporary France on his gift for the public spoken word—it will be twenty-seven years this coming Sunday since that eighteenth of June 1940, when, as an unknown, he singularly introduced himself to history by stating over the London BBC, *"Moi, Général de Gaulle, actuellement à Londres, j'invite les officiers et les soldats français ..."* —and because, in his unique, influential verbal style, he has been speaking on the air to millions of listeners ever since, his silence during the recent alarming Six-Day Israeli-Arab War attracted great attention. In the international confusions, power ploys, and mixed human affections or hatreds felt for Jews or for Arabs, plus left and right political emotions, all of which were influential on today's Catholic French mentality, the French people had to make up their minds for themselves as to what to think of it all. The only official guidance they received was slight and very second-hand, passed on by de Gaulle's minister of information after

[1] From article by Genêt, pseudonym of *The New Yorker's* Paris correspondent, Janet Flanner. *New Yorker*. 43:84+. Je. 24, '67. Excerpts from the article "Letter from Paris," by Genêt, reprinted by permission; © 1967 The New Yorker Magazine, Inc.

a Conseil des Ministres, presided over by de Gaulle himself. In the opening sample of this guidance, the Minister prolixly and tautologically divulged to the Paris press, "France is favorable to a basic settlement that will tend to lead to a true peace and to a settlement of the Israeli-Arab problems, and not to a mere sealing off of difficulties from making their appearance"—an idea that de Gaulle himself would certainly have stated with more enlightening clarity or else with much richer ambiguity. . . .

An influential source for further confusion and split in the French reaction on the Middle East war lay in the fact that the French Communists, who comprise about a fifth of the most politically minded portion of the population here, loyally followed the Soviet line and were thus pro-Nasser and pro-Arab. The rest of the French, possibly as a belated form of generalized European guilt felt for the fate of the masses of European Jews lost in the horrors of the German crematories, were overwhelmingly pro-Israel, especially after Nasser's insane promise to wipe Israel's two and a half million Jews off the earth of the Holy Land. . . . From Tel Aviv itself came the report that the Israelis were "very bitter at the neutrality of the French," with whom they thought they had enjoyed over the years an informal, friendly alliance that was still operative. Were the Egyptians at this moment in any shape to protest about anything at all, Paris Middle East experts suppose that Cairo, too, might well be complaining —in its case, about Moscow's failure to give any important support to the Arab cause during this last fortnight.

Israel's victory has, in spite of everything, been a piece of very good luck indeed for the Gaullist party, and certainly a stroke of good fortune for de Gaulle himself, since foreign affairs are his exclusive concern. And certainly his must have been the decisive voice in the only official statement of government policy made by the Conseil des Ministres, on June 2nd, when the war was about to break—"France is not committed, in any way or on any subject, to any of the states involved." Masses of Gaullists were shocked at what was immediately called his neutralization of France in a time of war between Israel and the Arabs, when the Gaullists felt that France could not, with morality, be neutral about the Jews. There was also the feeling on the part of most of the French that the escaped Jews, having made Israel their abode, should not be betrayed again, and this time by someone they had counted on to stand by them as a friend.

Apparently, the top Gaullist most familiar with de Gaulle's use of neutralism as a doctrinal resource was [the then] Premier Pompidou. He had already made a speech about it some time ago, doubtless at de Gaulle's demand and probably so as to put the idea into circulation without anyone's paying much attention to it, because de Gaulle wanted to insert it into history when the right time came. "In this dangerous world," Pompidou said in his speech, "in which the great powers have endless, incalculable strength at their disposal, there must be one voice that can be lifted for the right of nations, no matter how feeble they are, to answer for themselves and say what they want to say about their own destiny"—presumably, whether they get their wish or not. France has, it seems, on de Gaulle's decision, become that single voice, which will naturally give her a unique new importance, if anyone is listening. On de Gaulle's theory of neutralization, an explicit, if puzzling, article with the semi-ironic title "Why de Gaulle Dropped Israel" was published in last week's *Nouvel Observateur,* which analyzes the General's theories, beginning at the beginning: "After having disposed of the Algerian war, after having given independence to the major part of the French empire, de Gaulle's France could claim to have no more colonial or imperialistic ties, and could thus make herself the apostle of cooperation and represent *les petites nations,*" for whom no one normally speaks and who rarely get a chance to speak for themselves. In the world of the little nations, his doctrinaire neutralism seems to de Gaulle to be "the only manner of escape for them—and, indeed, for the entire world—from the blows that are dealt society by the power struggle between the Americans and the Soviet Union," whose "concerted hegemony is a yoke" equally to be resisted, if possible. In his pessimistic wisdom, the article adds, he feels that Russian-American agreements would be almost as dangerous for the world as Russian-American disagreements. . . .

DE GAULLE WOOS THE ARABS [2]

President de Gaulle is forging ahead with his efforts to make France the foremost Western power in the Arab world. His determination as well as his successes and temporary setbacks have recently been evident.

The French government . . . [in April 1968] signed an agreement permitting the Iraqi air force to obtain fifty-four ultramodern Mirage fighter-bombers similar to the fifty planes the French are denying to Israel even though the Israeli government has paid for them in full.

France [he said], is more than ever the friend of the Arabs, especially at this moment when their territory is being invaded. . . . Cooperation with the underdeveloped countries is one of the fundamental aspects of French foreign policy.

The French President is known to feel keenly that the United States and Britain have left a political vacuum in the Arab Middle East that can be filled only by the Soviet Union on one side and by France on the other.

The United States, in the general's view, will be kept for a long time from playing an active role in the Middle East, not only because the Arabs, like all countries of the Third World, are bitterly opposed to United States policies in Vietnam but more fundamentally because of the traditionally close ties between Israel and the United States. As for Britain, she is resigned, or condemned, according to the Gaullist view, to an increasingly secondary role in the area.

The French government, although its officials are not in the habit of saying so publicly, is as concerned as are other

[2] From article by Henry Tanner, staff correspondent. New York *Times.* p E4. Ap. 21, '68. © 1968 by The New York Times Company. Reprinted by permission.

Western powers over Soviet penetration of the Middle East and the spectacular surge of Soviet naval strength in the Mediterranean.

General de Gaulle strongly believes that the world can live peacefully only if the relative strength of the principal nations is balanced.

If he is preoccupied, or even obsessed, by the dangers of what he calls the American "hegemony" in world affairs, he would no less deplore a Soviet domination of the Arab Middle East and of Algeria. To him every imbalance anywhere has in it the seeds of conflict.

Ironically, the French-Iraqi agreement coincided with the announcement that exploitation of the northern Rumaila oil deposit, one of the richest in the world, would not be delegated to a foreign company but would be undertaken by the Iraqi government itself. The government-controlled French Oil Company had been the best-placed foreign bidder for the concession. The sharp disappointment that was felt in Paris over this decision was compounded by the fact that a French bid for a concession to exploit the important Misracq sulphur concession had also failed.

This raised the possibility that the sale of the fifty-four Mirages, which will cost about $70 million, might be financed by the French government in the form of military assistance rather than through a straight commercial deal with oil and mineral concessions as the *quid pro quo*.

Another possibility was that the Iraqis were holding out on Rumaila in the hope that the French would eventually offer them a different kind of deal—namely, a partnership between the Iraqi government and the French Oil Company. This is the basis on which the French have been operating in Algeria. . . .

Libya also could be a precedent in this sense. French petroleum interests moved into that country for the first time early this month. They did so in the form of a partnership with the Libyan government rather than an old-style concession. Libya, which last year was the world's seventh-largest oil producer, had long been the exclusive hunting ground of American and British oil interests.

Ever since the liquidation of the Algerian war lifted the terrible weight that had paralyzed French-Arab relations, General de Gaulle has patiently and methodically pursued the goal of building up French influence in the Arab world.

LETTER FROM WASHINGTON [3]

It can be unsettling to dwell upon what might be the state of this union today if dumb luck had not favored it in moments of great danger during the last two decades. In June 1950, a providential boycott of the Security Council by the Soviet Union made it possible for us to intervene in Korea as an agent of the United Nations. The Soviet representative was under orders to absent himself in protest against the presence of the Chinese Nationalists; had he been at his station, he would have vetoed the enabling resolution and thus compelled this country to abandon its intervention or, as we would almost certainly have done, to go on with it in disregard of the Security Council. Since then, the Russians have coexisted with the Chinese Nationalists in the UN and have not allowed pique or principle to get in the way of policy. However, their falling out with the Chinese Communists and the subsequent falling out of the Chinese leaders among themselves—developments that caught us by surprise and confounded many of our leading theoreticians—have so far worked very much to our advantage, at least in the sense of lessening the hazards of our unilateral intervention in Vietnam.

Now, in what may be the greatest stroke of luck in our recent history, we are the beneficiaries of the power and swiftness of maneuver of Israeli arms—or, as it might be seen through Russian eyes, of the vulnerability of Arab defenses

[3] From article by Richard H. Rovere, correspondent. *New Yorker.* 43:90+. Je. 24, '67. Excerpts from the article "Letter from Washington" by Richard H. Rovere, reprinted by permission; © 1967 The New Yorker Magazine, Inc.

and the incompetence of the Egyptian High Command. No one here thinks that we could have avoided some kind of military involvement if the war had gone on for more than a week or two, or if there had been at any point a period of a few days in which the outcome was in doubt. The President had made nonintervention an aim of American policy and had so advised the Soviet premier, who had replied that it was also the aim of his government. But the road to war in this century has been littered with such assurances. Moreover, Soviet nonintervention, as it had been explained to the Arab leaders, was contingent on American nonintervention, which in practice would almost certainly have been contingent on Israel's capacity for achieving an early superiority and maintaining it for the duration. Had there not been a large gap in the Egyptian radar net, and had not the Israelis learned of it and exploited it at the outset with the Mystère fighter-bombers they had been fortunate enough to be able to purchase from the nonaligned French, we would have faced, perhaps in the first week of combat, what would have appeared to be a clear choice between the defense of Israel, on the one hand, and, on the other, an acceptance of its destruction and of Soviet dominance throughout the Middle East. At the same time, the Soviets would have had to choose between nonintervention and the wrecking of the most audacious of their diplomatic designs. As things worked out, we had no need and they had no time to reconsider. . . .

Solving the U. S. Dilemma

The war may have solved more problems for the Johnson Administration here than for the Eshkol Administration in Tel Aviv, which, partly as a consequence of its efforts to please and accommodate the United States, is said to face a formidable challenge from its opposition. As soon as it was clear that Israeli armor was meeting little resistance as it moved across the Sinai, the President had nothing to do except instruct Ambassador Goldberg to plead for a cease-fire in the Security Council and to be expediently long-winded about it; it was an assignment perfectly suited to the Ambassador's talents and to the political needs of the Administration, at home as well as abroad. ...

We entered the crisis with nothing worthy of description as a policy, and it can hardly be said that we have one now. We will agree with everyone else that border questions should not be settled by force of arms, but such agreement is meaningless in this situation, and there is hardly anyone here who would not be delighted if the Israelis could manage to hold on to whatever territories they have seized and that are, in their view, necessary for the country's security. We will defend the Israeli position that the best chance of a lasting settlement lies in agreements reached by the recent belligerents themselves. But if anything is clear at the moment, it is that several Arab governments will have to fall and be replaced before any of them will concede Israel's legitimacy. ...

The only hope that anyone can see right now is that in time we can persuade the Soviets that their interests in the Middle East and ours are pretty much the same.

V. THE NEW POWER BALANCE

EDITOR'S INTRODUCTION

In his search for a balance of power in the Middle East, General de Gaulle looks, through the medium of France, to prevent what all the Western powers fear—the preponderance of Soviet power that would bring the Middle East into the Russian sphere of influence. There is no doubt that the Soviets envisage at long last the strategic positions on the Mediterranean Sea and Indian Ocean they have long sought.

The danger, as Walter Laqueur, director of the Institute of Contemporary History in London, points out in the last selection, is that the Middle East could turn into another Vietnam. The intervention of other powers in order to create a balance of power is itself hazardous. Moreover, in the Soviet view, the next round in the continuing Arab-Israeli conflict should go to the Arabs; but this might well prove impossible without direct Russian involvement. Any such engagement with the open support of the Soviets could easily develop into a contest between the two superpowers, with no way of predicting the end result of such an escalation.

The West is on notice that the balance of power is changing in the Middle East, and for this reason a clear, concerted policy by the Western powers is badly needed.

CHANGING THE GUARD [1]

Great Britain did not recover its primacy of influence east of the Mediterranean after the Suez episode [in 1956]. Before and for some years after World War II, Britain possessed a veritable chain of air, ground and naval bases throughout

[1] From the article "Changing of the Guard in the Middle East," by the late Halford L. Hoskins, dean of the Fletcher School of Law and Diplomacy in Medford, Massachusetts, and author of *The Middle East. Current History.* 52:65-6+. F. '67. Reprinted by permission of the author's estate and of Current History, Inc.

the Mediterranean, a chain supplemented by French positions and, for a brief period, by those of the United States. At one time or another after World War II, the three powers possessed or held treaty rights at as many as forty-three bases approachable from the Mediterranean. For various reasons, outgrowths generally of nationalist influences, nearly all these positions were withdrawn from Western use within eight years after the close of World War II. Quite aside from this trend, which saw both Malta and Cyprus emerge as independent states and Gibraltar exposed to contest by Spain, Britain failed, for economic reasons, to recover its dominant position in the Mediterranean. In late years, except for vast technological improvements relating to the propulsion of surface and subsea vessels, the range and armament of missiles, the range and effectiveness of planes from aircraft carriers, and logistical arrangements enabling vessels to remain at sea indefinitely without recourse to fixed bases, the Middle East might have luxuriated in a political vacuum practically immune from great-power interference. Neither Britain nor France could muster the financial resources necessary for remaining at the top level of efficiency in armament and only the United States, among the Western powers, possessed the wealth and facilities requisite for the maintenance of power —minus bases—in the western approaches to the Middle East. In view of the recent buildup of Soviet naval strength in the Mediterranean, it remains to be seen whether the United States, with the newer forms of equipment, has adequately filled the vacuum left by the diminishing of British and French power in the area.

The maintenance of Western influence in the Middle East has by no means depended on the strength and visibility of military equipment alone. As the postwar concept of defense through containment gave place to deterrence laced with international competition, the uses of various types of aid as an adjunct to diplomacy were seen to be not only desirable but mandatory. In this respect, after World War II the United States possessed a capability well above the combined resources of its European allies. The Soviet bloc was also unable to compete on even terms in monetary outlay. By the year 1965, the total value of United States aid of various kinds extended to countries of the Middle East (including Egypt) since World War II amounted conservatively to not less than $8 billion. It is difficult to assess the effects of this outlay, apart from other influences. Both Israel and Jordan were enabled to survive as individual states. At the same time, there was a growing cordiality in the relations of Turkey and Iran with the Soviet Union despite the application in these countries of United States aid valued at $4 billion and $1.5 billion respectively. Clearly, the influences that have been flowing into the Middle East in late years have not all been Western.

British Withdrawals

If the confrontation of rival power systems on the Mediterranean exposure of the Middle East might occasion some apprehension in Western capitals, the situation east of Suez surely has been no more reassuring. When Britain and the four Middle Eastern members of the Baghdad Pact* (later CENTO)—along with United States observers—were completing their defense organization late in 1955, they did not seem to anticipate that measures would also have to be taken to guard approaches to the Middle East from the Arabian Sea. Danger did not then appear to lurk in that quarter. While difficulties of various kinds abounded in Aden, Britain had given no serious thought to the abandonment of that strategic post. Indeed, plans were being laid for the construction there of one of the largest oil refineries east of Suez. At that period, Britain still maintained sovereign authority at points on the east African coast and Egyptian interference with Suez Canal operations had not yet become very disturbing. In postwar years, Britain had become dependent on Persian Gulf oil for the greater part of its energy require-

* The Baghdad Pact, signed in 1955 by the United Kingdom, Iran, Iraq, Pakistan and Turkey, became known as the Central Treaty Organization (CENTO) after the withdrawal of Iraq in 1959.

ments. Principally for this reason, a small post had been established on the island of Bahrein, whence surveillance could be extended over much of the gulf area.

In 1961, British responsibilities in the Gulf were put to the test. Shortly after a new British-Kuwaiti accord had been announced, attesting to Kuwait's independence and redefining Britain's protective role, Premier Abdul Karim Kassem of Iraq seized the opportunity to publicize a claim that Kuwait remained an integral part of the Iraqi province of Basra, declaring that "the era of sheikhdoms is over." His obvious objective drew immediate response from several sources, each with its own type of concern. Egypt's Nasser, aware of Kuwait's application for membership in the Arab League, expectant of largesse from Kuwait's ample resources, and suspicious of Kassem's designs in the Persian Gulf, gave voice in opposition before relapsing into sulky silence, presumably because of great-power pressure which could not be disregarded. Saudi Arabia, which could adduce its own historic claim to Kuwait, gave assurance of its support of the sheikhdom's independence. Iran dismissed the Iraqi claim as ludicrous. The United States advised the Iraqi government to avoid the use of force in pressing its claim.

Britain reacted the more calmly, because of its interest in the Iraq Petroleum Company whose relations with the Iraqi regime had seemed to be improving. Britain was not slow, nevertheless, in manifesting readiness to defend the sheikhdom. While Kuwait mobilized its own miniscule forces, British troops, tanks and jet planes were landed at Kuwait at the sheikh's request and other forces in Kenya, Aden and Bahrein were placed on alert. At the United Nations Security Council it became apparent that Iraq was receiving encouragement from the Soviet Union. Soviet insistence that the upbuilding of British forces in Kuwait and the assembling of naval units had created a "crisis" threatened to make a major international issue of what had begun as little more than an unpleasant regional incident.

The replacement of British forces in Kuwait with units from several of the Arab states, with Britain obviously less than anxious to continue in its former role as keeper of the peace, brought into open view the limits of Western-engineered pacts for Middle East security. That a Western power structure was needed east of Suez was made apparent not so much by the loss of positions of strength in the Mediterranean as by the easterly trend of Egyptian designs under Soviet sponsorship, Iraqi-Iranian clashes over navigation rights in the Shaat-al-Arab, increasing restiveness in Iran, and growing assertiveness of oil-wealthy Persian Gulf sheikhdoms. Moreover, since the reopening of the Suez Canal in 1957, ready access from the West to South Arabia and the Persian Gulf was no longer assured. It is true that Egypt had not impeded passage through the canal of British armed vessels and personnel despatched for the defense of Kuwait in 1961. But, in view of other restrictions placed on the use of the canal when Egyptian interests might be involved, persistent reports that the Soviet Union was seeking from Egypt a concession for one or more naval stations in the Red Sea, the steady growth of the Soviet naval presence in the Mediterranean with increasingly sophisticated units, and reported Soviet influence in the armed forces of Syria, Iraq, Egypt, Algeria and possibly even Cyprus, there could be no certainty that the Suez Canal would be available for use on other and perhaps graver occasions. . . .

With British manpower in short supply, foreign exchange overstrained and devaluation of the pound sterling a distinct possibility, Britain saw no escape from the necessity of withdrawing completely from the area east of Suez unless the United States was prepared to underwrite most of the cost of new installations and provisions for their defense. The British view was taken with more reluctance because of the manifest truth in the adage that "he who pays the piper calls the tune."

These developments placed the United States in something of a quandary. The newly-surveyed route of passage obviously was essential if ever the power vacuum adjoining the underbelly of the Middle East were to be filled, and a safe line of transit to the farther east established. Yet a steady rise in the cost of war in Vietnam, far beyond defense commitments in the Middle East and elsewhere, left little range of choice. In July 1966, the United States suggested that the British might as well cut their forces east of Suez since they no longer served a useful purpose. To what extent the political vacuum in the western Indian Ocean may be filled remains an open question. As to the changing of the guard, however, there can be no question.

THE ARAB WORLD: SOVIET ROLE WIDENS [2]

The Soviet Union, in a move that underlines its strengthened strategic role in the Mediterranean and in the Arab world, has arranged to post technicians in Mers-el-Kebir, the former French base in western Algeria, 260 miles from the Strait of Gibraltar. . . .

The Soviet presence so near Gibraltar alarms some Western and Arab officials because it is regarded as establishing Moscow's political influence in an area where Spain and Britain are at odds and where Morocco and Algeria carry on an old quarrel over frontiers.

The military significance of the move, according to Western and Arab sources, whose planning must include the possibility of a major Soviet-Western confrontation, is that a Soviet force at Mers-el-Kebir would have the capacity—a carrier is to be added to the Soviet Mediterranean fleet—to block the strait and deny some Western navies access to the Mediterranean. . . .

Steady Soviet Growth

The spread of military power in terms of *de facto* naval and air bases and the establishment of a Mediterranean fleet is only one aspect of the steady growth of Soviet influence

[2] From one of a series of articles by Drew Middleton, staff correspondent. New York *Times.* p 1+. Jl. 16, '68. © 1968 by The New York Times Company. Reprinted by permission.

among the Arab nations since the war of June 1967, in which the United Arab Republic and Syria, two Soviet clients, were defeated, along with Jordan, by Israel.

The Soviet Union is regarded generally as the paramount foreign influence in Iraq, Algeria and the Sudan, as well as in Egypt and Syria. Soviet commercial and aid missions are active in Morocco, Tunisia and Kuwait.

The Communist party is proscribed in the Arab world. The Soviet Union has not sought to end the proscription or to establish powerful underground parties, preferring to work through underground groups hostile to the regimes in such non-Socialist countries as Jordan, Libya, Saudi Arabia and Kuwait. . . .

The predominant feeling among Western and Arab observers in the area is that the Russians have altered the strategic situation at the crossroads of Europe, Africa and Asia to the marked disadvantage of the United States.

Those sources make these points:

1. The Soviet Union is in a geographical position that would enable its political and military forces to bring pressure on the Arab oil-producing nations to halt the flow of oil to Western Europe in any Middle East crisis. Western Europe gets most of its oil from the Arab countries, whose reserves were estimated in 1966 at 223 million barrels, or about 57 per cent of the world total.

2. By establishing naval facilities from Latakia westward, the Soviet Union has turned the southern flank of the North Atlantic Treaty Organization. The original NATO strategic conception was that its naval power in the Mediterranean would discourage Soviet penetration there.

3. By supplying arms to Syria, Iraq, the United Arab Republic, the Sudan and Algeria, followed by the introduction of Soviet instructors and technicians, Moscow has built a powerful influence among the armed forces of a region where those forces are customarily the determinants of political power.

Soviet political influence, in the view of the majority of moderate Arab leaders and of American and other diplomats, will be used to maintain the "revolutionary situation" in the area. Non-Socialist Arab leaders console themselves with the conviction that Moscow would not dare risk a confrontation with the United States. They do not believe the Russians would support militarily a "war of national liberation" were one to erupt in an Arab country if such support could lead to a showdown with the United States.

The Soviet Union suffered a military reverse in the defeat in June 1967 of the Arabs it had armed. It suffered a diplomatic defeat at the United Nations a month later when pro-Arab resolutions it had inspired were rejected.

Capitalizing on the War

How were the Russians able to transform defeat into a fulfillment of the centuries-old dream of a foothold in the Mediterranean? They capitalized on two results of the war.

First there was the shock of humiliating defeat on the Arabs and their need for an understanding friend. Second, there was hostility toward the United States as a result of its support in arms and diplomacy for Israel before the war and President Gamal Abdel Nasser's assertion—later retracted by the Egyptians—that American planes had helped the Israeli Air Force in the fighting itself.

Moscow moved rapidly. An airlift of more than eight hundred flights replenished most of the lost arms of the United Arab Republic and Syria. Officers and technicians entered these and other countries to train the armies in the new weapons.

Economic diplomacy was accelerated. Arab nations were offered barter deals for their primary products. Such deals are atractive to governments chronically short of foreign exchange.

Soviet technical aid to industry, agriculture and social services was expanded. The program in the Soviet Union for the education of Arabs was increased. Cultural ties were strengthened.

In contrast to their first efforts in the 1950's, the Russians this time went beyond the "progressive" countries. Royalist Morocco, for example, among America's oldest friends in Africa, was courted by the new diplomacy.

Since June 1967, according to officials in Rabat, the Soviet Union has established a Consulate General in Casablanca, contributed to the building of several dams, agreed to construct a thermoelectric plant, offered to help build an internal airline with Soviet equipment and negotiated a "very favorable" commercial agreement with Morocco. Moscow has also facilitated Morocco's purchase of $16 million worth of arms, mostly tanks and field artillery, from Czechoslovakia.

Soviet diplomacy has been quick and adaptable. Because of the recent strikes in France, Morocco faced the loss of forty tons of oranges already aboard ship, but the Soviet Union saved the day with an offer to purchase the cargo.

A less open but equally intensive Soviet campaign is reported to be going on. French, British and American intelligence sources say there is a substantial flow of Soviet funds to editors, party leaders, teachers and key military personnel.

The United Arab Republic is the mainspring of Soviet influence. From their central position in the most populous of Arab nations, the Russians have been able to move south into the Sudan, where they are reequipping and training the army.

According to neighboring leaders, President Nasser's independence is rapidly disappearing.

One experienced intelligence operative said that he "knew" that Ambassador Sergei A. Vinogradov had rejected an effort by the Egyptian leader to renew full diplomatic relations with the United States earlier this year.

"What else can Nasser do?" asked a Tunisian diplomat. His and other estimates agreed that 60 per cent of Egyptian trade is with the Soviet Union and Eastern Europe. These nations buy 70 per cent of the cotton crop, Egypt's main source of foreign exchange, and supply 80 per cent of her food imports, primarily wheat.

The military revival of the United Arab Republic and Syria has provided the Soviet Union with free entry for its own forces. To date, Cairo has been given about 250 jet fighters and 90 bombers. About 300 Egyptian pilots have been trained in the Soviet Union to fly MIG-21's.

About 3,000 Soviet officers have come to Egypt to train the armed forces. These include 70 to 100 Soviet pilots who fly with the Egyptians and, according to qualified sources, sometimes on missions of their own to familiarize themselves with the area. There also are between 30 and 40 Soviet pilots in Syria.

The expanded instructional program has enabled the Russians to assume increasing control in a key area: the selection of officers for promotion. That control has carried with it in Egypt and Syria a capacity for molding the armed forces.

Egyptian officers, however, still scandalize their mentors by continuing to play polo at the Gezira Club in Cairo. The discipline of the Red Army is not for Egyptian youth.

"These Russians are the limit," an Egyptian pilot wrote his mother from the air force base at Mersa Matruh, "they keep us with the planes day and night. One flight has to sleep with the planes. And they even make us fly at night."

Some Arab officials, notably in Algeria and Egypt, profess confidence that the Arab nations will "use" the Russians for political and economic aid as long as their aid is needed and then will be in a position to ease them out. Few Western diplomats agreed with this forecast.

MORE DANGEROUS THAN VIETNAM [3]

It is now almost a year since the outbreak of the Middle Eastern crisis which led to the third Arab-Israeli war. But even now it is not at all clear whether it was a mere episode in a long-drawn-out conflict or a decisive turning point. On the surface it seems as if nothing at all has changed since before the war: President Gamal Abdel Nasser of Egypt still says that he will not negotiate with Israel; Mohammed Heikal, his chief unofficial spokesman, again claims that war with Israel is inevitable. King Faisal of Saudi Arabia has been calling for a holy war and the Syrians for a people's war. The Israelis have engaged in massive retaliation against terrorist attacks. The refugees are still in their hovels and the Russians still supply arms to the Arabs.

Gradually, the world has reconciled itself to the idea that there will be a fourth Arab-Israeli war in the not-too-distant future. Despite the efforts of Dr. Gunnar Jarring, the Swedish diplomat who has been representing Secretary General Thant in the Mideast, it was doubtful from the beginning whether his mission ever had a real chance. The Arab leaders have refused as a matter of principle to recognize Israel by meeting her representatives face to face. A few Arabs now realize that it might have been a mistake not to talk to the Jews: It is one of the ironies of history that, but for this intransigence, the Jewish state would probably never have come into existence or, at most, have been confined to a small stretch of land in the coastal plain between Tel Aviv and Haifa; in negotiation, the Zionists would have settled for much less than they eventually got.

How near, then, is a new war? Last year the air forces of the Arab countries were wiped out by Israel, which also destroyed or captured some eight hundred tanks and hundreds of pieces of artillery. These losses were replaced by the

[3] From "The Middle East Is Potentially More Dangerous than Vietnam," by Walter Laqueur, director of the Institute of Contemporary History in London and professor of politics at Brandeis University. New York *Times Magazine.* p 34-5+. My. 5, '68. © 1968 by The New York Times Company. Reprinted by permission.

Russians, who have supplied to the Arabs some of their latest
and most sophisticated arms, such as the SU-7 fighter-bomber,
heavy bombers and long-distance ground-to-ground rockets.
Many military experts believe that it will nevertheless take
years for the Egyptians to retrain their forces and that, geo-
graphically, Israel is now in a much better position vis-à-vis
both Egypt and Syria than last year: Israeli forces literally
look down on Egypt from the Suez Canal and on Syria from
the Golan Heights. The experts conclude, therefore, that the
Arab states are less ready for a war than last year, and that
Israel is even stronger than in 1967. But wars do not necessarily break out when one or both sides in a conflict have
attained that stage of minimum readiness which the generals
demand; last year's war, according to this logic, should never
have happened. It occurred not because the Arabs were ready
but because they were impatient.

Nasser's Staying Power

Now the internal pressures in the Arab world are even
stronger and the international situation even more fraught
with dangers. President Nasser has shown amazing staying
power over the years, but his political survival is now very
much in doubt. Many hundreds of Egyptian officers and
about three hundred senior police and intelligence officials
have been ousted; fifty-four were brought to trial in January.
They may have been remiss in their duties, but there is no
good reason to assume that their successors will be more
efficient or loyal. The revelations in their trials have been
damaging: Shamseddin Badran, who was war minister when
the fighting began last June and one of the defendants in
the January trials, said he knew in May that there were no
Israeli troop concentrations—that the Russians and the
Syrians, in other words, had misled Cairo. Nasser, it transpired, had been warned by the Americans that Israel might
attack and had been asked by his own military command, now
under arrest or in disgrace, to attack first, but had refused
to do so.

After the "setback," as Cairo describes the war, Nasser promised an "open society"—more freedom and social reform, less dead wood, more honesty and realism. But Egyptian society is no more open now than it was a year ago. Nor has Egyptian domestic propaganda changed. Nasser's statements for foreign consumption are still heavily doctored for publication inside Egypt. The field of publicity still is—to quote a remarkable essay in *Encounter* by Cecil Hourani, the Arab intellectual—"in the hands of professional demagogues, blackmailers and semieducated fanatics." In the first flush of self-criticism, resolutions were made to view the world more realistically and to refrain from extreme emotionalism: not to insist on the annihilation of Israel because it embarrassed even the Russians, not to continue publishing the "Protocols of Zion," the anti-Semitic forgery of the 1890's, but to differentiate between good Jews and bad Zionists. By now most of these good intentions have been forgotten.

Egyptian relations with Britain and France have been mended. But when a *rapprochement* with the United States, however modest in scope, was proposed, it immediately faced stiff resistance. Heikal, the editor of the influential newspaper *Al Ahram,* wrote that Egypt, the matador, should not tackle the American bull head-on but outmaneuver it with skillful tactics. A strong faction, however, does not want to outmaneuver America, but to bury it. In March, workers and students rioted for several days; "Wake up, oh Nasser," they shouted, "restore civil liberties! Bomb the Jews in Sinai! Down with the Arab reactionaries!" (They also shouted: "Down with the mendacious Heikal!") Some of them were Communists of various ideological persuasions, others members of the illegal Muslim Brotherhood; the majority were simply discontented young men and women. Last June, after the defeat, they had demonstrated to induce Nasser to withdraw his resignation. Now, less than a year later, the crowds demand the redemption of Nasser's pledges. They are asking him to do the impossible: He cannot attack the "reactionaries," for the kings and emirs are keeping the Egyptian economy afloat; the yearly subsidy of $266 million to compensate Cairo for the end of the Suez Canal revenues and other losses is paid by Saudi Arabia, Kuwait and Libya. To throw the Israelis out of Sinai is easier said than done for the moment. The restoration of political freedom in Egypt would mean the end of the regime. Nasser said at a workers' meeting that the demand for "freedom" was a counterrevolutionary slogan; for the worker freedom meant that he had a job, and for the student, that he could go to college.

Urban Egypt is too sophisticated for such arguments. Everyone knows that after years of promises of social reform, economic growth and military glory, there is more austerity than ever before and Israeli soldiers camp at the gates of Suez and Port Said. Eventually, however, the demonstrations did have an effect; a program of political reform was announced in late March, guaranteeing full individual liberty, a permanent constitution and, once Israel withdraws from the occupied territories, free parliamentary and presidential elections. But Nasser has no intention of relinquishing power or abolishing the one-party system. For this reason, if no other, there is no evidence to indicate that the new announcements will be of any greater significance than similar promises in the past.

Soviet Pressures

Since last June, Egypt has been the scene of a constant tug-of-war between the "Russian party," those in favor of closer ties to the Soviet Union, and other factions. For the moment the "Russians" have prevailed, but their hold is by no means firm. . . . The influence of this group grew as the Soviet Union got more and more involved in Egypt; more than half of Egypt's foreign trade is now with the Eastern bloc and several thousand Soviet military and civilian advisers help to direct Egypt's war effort, its industrial production and its intelligence services. But the Russian faction is resented by most Egyptian technocrats and intellectuals and many army officers. On the left it has to compete against

Chinese, Cuban and Algerian influences. Above all, it has hardly any support among the masses. . . .

The position of the army is weaker now, and the Russians are pressing for some form of popular democracy to replace the remnants of the "military bourgeoisie," as they call the "new class" that has emerged during the last fifteen years. Nasser has tried to keep a balance between left and right, but he is again the prisoner of his own promises, more so than last June. Pressure is growing all the time to renew the war against Israel; the "setback" is intolerable, and Arab honor should immediately be restored. Nasser knows that he is not ready for war, but he is also aware that in ancient Rome there was a very short distance from the Capitol to the Tarpeian Rock, where politicians who had failed were executed.

For several months the question of how to wage war against Israel has been discussed all over the Arab world. Nasser's friends have argued that only the regular armies of the Arab states will be in a position to administer a decisive blow to Israel. Since the armies are not yet ready and fully coordinated, they say, the strategy to pursue vis-à-vis Israel is one of "neither peace nor war," a policy of nonbelligerent attrition which would weaken Israel's economy and undermine its confidence. As Heikal recently wrote: "Without any effort on our part, we were near [success] at the time of the Israeli economic depression in 1966; at that time emigration from Israel exceeded immigration." Israel, this school of thought argues, is neither Vietnam nor Algeria—the Jewish state would retaliate to Vietcong-style attacks by expelling the Arab minority. On the other hand, the Syrians, the Palestine refugee organizations and various pro-Castro and pro-Mao factions maintain that the Vietcong experience shows that guerrilla warfare can defeat "imperialism" anywhere and should be applied in the Middle East, too. Nasser and the Soviet leaders have disputed this, but American setbacks in Vietnam no doubt make the idea of a guerrilla war much more popular.

Guerrilla warfare will not work against Israel, but all the evidence seems to show that it will be tried on a much greater scale than hitherto. Many hundreds of guerrillas are being trained in camps in Syria and Jordan; such Vietcong tactics as the firing of small rockets from jeeps or other mobile bases have been applied in Israel in recent weeks. The quality of the attacks has been mostly poor so far; it will no doubt improve in coming months. Even so, conditions from the Arab point of view are not favorable. In his works on guerrilla warfare, Mao attributes decisive importance to factors such as the existence of an extensive territory, a lack of communications in the hinterland, the numerical insufficiency of enemy troops, the absence of airborne units. All these factors do not exist in Israel, a small country in which there is nowhere to hide. Che Guevara and Régis Debray insisted that the first objective of a guerrilla war is to destroy enemy forces. The Arab partisans concentrate on laying landmines; they cannot confront regular army units. The further stages of guerrilla warfare à la Guevara and Debray, such as the establishment of bases in enemy territory and carrying the battle to enemy strongholds, are thus ruled out. Arab guerrillas do not face the Kuomintang, Algerian colons [French settlers] or a banana republic; they threaten with destruction not a small ruling class, but a modern state with the people solidly behind it.

Hit and Run

The Arab guerrillas cannot create bases inside Israel. Their main hope is to exploit an irredenta along the cease-fire line and to organize hit-and-run attacks from across the border. Such a strategy cannot have great returns: a few tractors will be mined, a few pumping stations destroyed and a few civilians killed or wounded each week. There may be a few more spectacular instances of individual terror. This policy will make life uncomfortable for the Israelis living near the border, but it has never been very peaceful in this area anyway. For those who have lived in Israel or Palestine during the last thirty years, riots, nighttime attacks and low-key guerrilla warfare have been the normal state of affairs.

Hit-and-run attacks have the effect of provoking Israel into massive retaliation, and this could be their purpose. Major Israeli retaliatory actions are an embarrassment, even to Israel's friends in the West. The Arabs expect that Western pressure will be put on the Israeli "hawks" not to engage in massive retaliation even if this restraint should produce more frequent and more destructive Arab raids. It is unlikely, to put it mildly, that Israel will accept this argument, however strong the pressure exerted. In the eyes of the Israeli military and political leaders, such a policy would be suicidal. They do not wish to embarrass their friends, but even less do they want to commit suicide. The policy of goading Israel into massive retaliation will therefore have the expected short-term results for the Arabs. But stepping up guerrilla infiltration will almost inevitably result in Israeli counteraction, hitting with greater strength at guerrilla bases deep in Arab territory. This the Arab governments will not be able to stand. There will be public clamor for a "fourth round now," and we know from last year's experience what is likely to happen after that.

During his long political career, Nasser has shown virtues infrequent among Arab statesman—great daring coupled with caution and persistence, fortitude at a time when things went against him. He has displayed supreme tactical skill, time and again outsmarting his opponents. Not a very effective speaker himself, he has provided his country with a most impressive propaganda apparatus. Hard-working, incorruptible, dynamic, he has symbolized for many foreigners the spirit of the new Egypt. Only a few close observers were aware of the reverse of the coin: the irrational streak in his behavior, the indifference to moral principle, the absence of a sense of moderation, the overwhelming ambition, the belief that he could tackle everything at the same time—social reform, industrial expansion, the Aswan dam, Arab unity, rockets, construction of jet planes, a not-so-little war in Yemen, a campaign against other Arab rulers, full-scale war against Israel. The country was too poor and too small for such great ambitions.

Egypt's problems are very nearly insoluble. Under sober, purposeful and very modest leadership, the country could probably have made some progress; but the expectations aroused by the "revolutionary regime" were far too great to be satisfied by, at best, slow advance. Egypt and the whole Arab world were to regain their past glory, but the gap between ambition and performance widened all the time. That may well be Nasser's undoing. If Nasser disappears, the problems facing Egypt will remain, and for that reason the question of succession is not really of decisive importance. . . .

Hussein's Plight

King Hussein's plight is even more acute than Nasser's: He has tried to curb the activities of Al Fatah, a terrorist organization, but has been overruled by his ministers and the army officers. The Palestine irregulars have now established themselves as a private army in Jordan over which the King has no control, and they have taken over areas along the border with Israel. This would be an unhealthy state of affairs in any country at any time, and it means that the King is no longer a free agent. The Israelis hoped for a long time that they could reach an agreement wtih him; now they have no more such expectations, and whether Hashemite rule survives in Jordan is for them a matter of indifference. Al Fatah wants to keep Hussein, at least for the time being; he still has influential friends in the West, and an Egyptian-style or Syrian-style regime in Jordan would not get the military or financial help he is likely to obtain. But the King has lost effective control over the armed forces in his country, and Jordan, which in the past was an element of stability in the Middle East, has now become the center of the tension and possibly the focus of a new conflagration.

The Marquis D'Argenson is said to have observed a long time ago that there is nothing so dreadful as a great victory—

except, of course, a great defeat. The Israeli victory has not brought the country any nearer to its long-term goal, peace with the Arab world. The Israelis were totally unprepared for the magnitude of the victory and its consequences. Excellent improvisers, they established within a very short time an administration of the occupied territories that functions on the whole efficiently, humanely and inobtrusively. It is also perhaps a little too didactic and overeager to help and to fraternize, which does not always go down very well. The Israelis built new highways, sent physicians and nurses where they were needed, showed West Bank farmers how to use fertilizers and insecticide and how to improve agricultural yields. Though there have been exceptions, as an occupation army they have generally been a model of restraint. But military occupation is an unnatural state of affairs; however well behaved the Israeli soldiers, their presence is still resented by all those who simply do not want to live under Israeli rule.

At first everyone regarded the new situation as provisional, the occupied territories as a dead pledge to be given up after the peace treaty. *Rien ne dure que le provisoire* [Nothing lasts but the temporary]. Soon it appeared that there would be no peace: Nasser, after some initial muttering about the possibility of a "political solution," made it clear that only force could solve the Middle Eastern deadlock. The Syrians had said so from the beginning.

Within a few weeks, Israel declared that it would not withdraw unless its security was guaranteed and free access assured in the Gulf of Aqaba and the Suez Canal. A growing number of Israelis came to believe that since the Arab leaders were not willing to negotiate, rejecting the very idea of peace, the occupied areas should be made a part of the Jewish state. A Greater Israel movement emerged. Signatures were collected and appeals published in the press in favor of annexation; the government was bombarded with manifestos and warnings—not to surrender an inch, not to waver and procrastinate but to establish facts. The movement scored a success when the Minister of the Interior, Haim Moshe Shapiro, announced, quite unnecessarily, several measures which made it appear that the occupied areas would be incorporated into Israel. Abba Eban, the Foreign Minister, is the group's particular *bête noire;* he seems to symbolize a spirit of compromise in a situation in which, the advocates of annexation feel, a hard line is the only one likely to succeed.

The argument that Israel should not surrender any territory while the Arab countries refuse to talk peace is intelligible, but the ideological embellishments about historical rights are somewhat disquieting. A case for a Greater Israel could be made only on the basis of a binational state. Had the Israeli Government declared the day after victory that the character of the state was to change radically—that the Arabs would be equal citizens in every respect, that they would be represented on all levels of government and administration, including the very highest, according to their share in the population—such an appeal might have evoked a positive response. Whether it would have worked is more than doubtful: the binational experience is an unhappy one in such countries as Canada and Belgium, and it is working not too well even in Switzerland. Politically and psychologically, at any rate, Israel is not yet ready for such radical change. True, the Zionist phase of Israel is about to end or already over; the Arab fears of mass immigration are misplaced. The Zionist mystique born out of the suffering and longing of East European Jewry is gradually being replaced by a different concept of modern statehood as the first native-born generation takes over the political and military leadership. But the implications of statehood, the realization that a modern state cannot be run on the traditional Zionist lines, is dawning only gradually. There is resistance against such changes as the inevitable separation between state and religion.

What Price Peace

Israeli occupation policy has been to impress the Arabs that it is, to quote Moshe Dayan, the defense minister, "easy

to live under the occupation and difficult to undermine it."
The Israeli military, who are in effective control of the occupied areas, have few illusions. The Arab population wants
them to withdraw; the Arabs have not become loyal citizens
just because the Israeli government has brought better sanitation to their cities and better irrigation to the farms. A
young Arab patriot will support the guerrillas in the same
way a young Jew in Mandatory Palestine joined the Haganah, the Jewish military organization during the British
mandate. When Arab village elders promised Dayan that
they would accept responsibility for the young men in their
midst, the Israeli minister told them that he was not impressed: "Do you think the *Mukhtar* (Mayor) of Nahalal
knew what I was doing when I was a young man?" Dayan does
not expect loyalty; he simply assumes that the guerrillas and
their potential supporters will gradually realize that their sac-
rifice is pointless because they cannot destroy the state, and
that the only solution will be negotiations and peace. Sometimes the Israelis have shown a heavy hand—in destroying the
homes of terrorists or those who sheltered them or in exiling
Arab politicians who refused to collaborate with the authorities. The Israeli reply to criticism is invariably that an ounce
of prevention is better than a pound of cure.

Both the West Bank and the Gaza region are economic
liabilities; Gaza cannot support its 150,000 inhabitants, let
alone the 200,000 refugees still there. But these are not overwhelming difficulties. Israel could live with them for many
years, perhaps decades; nor do the problems of defense and
security constitute an impossible burden. The political issue
remains the central one: What price peace and security?

The Israeli government has been split about the future of
the occupied territories, much more so than the public. No
over-all plan has evolved; the question of peace has, wisely
perhaps, been left open. There has been talk about an Israeli-
Jordanian co-dominion over the West Bank, but this seems
no more viable than an Arab-Israeli federation.

Have any opportunities been missed by the Israelis? It seemed at one stage that Nasser would be willing to negotiate and that King Hussein only waited for a sign from Cairo to start dealing with the Israelis himself. American and British diplomats have maintained that Israel made it difficult for Nasser by insisting on direct negotiation, and President Tito of Yugoslavia has suggested that an "arrangement" could be reached even without negotiations—an unrecognized peace or at least a truce. The Israelis have been skeptical; there have been too many arrangements in the past that were discarded, including the one about freedom of shipping in the Gulf of Aqaba which led to last year's war. They have suggested to Dr. Jarring that they would be willing to accept the procedure used during the armistice negotiations at Rhodes in 1948. Then as now, the Arabs, refusing to talk to the Israelis, would deal only with the UN mediator, Dr. Ralph Bunche. (After two days they relented and direct talks took place between the two sides.) But Nasser immediately turned down the idea of using the 1948 rules again.

The Israelis have reluctantly reached the conclusion that the Arab leaders want a fourth round, not peace, and that peaceful statements are made to Western diplomats occasionally simply to gain time. For in political assemblies in Egypt, and more recently in meetings with army officers and soldiers in camps near the Suez Canal, Nasser has explained that only a new war would bring a decision, that everyone should prepare for this last, decisive battle. Nasser also said that it would take a little longer for the new Egyptian army to get ready for the battle. No exact timetable has been given, but he seems to believe that by 1970 at the latest the Egyptian army will have mastered the new weapons and be ready for war. The Israelis have to decide, as they had to last spring, whether to take these statements seriously. Some of Nasser's friends in the West have argued that the Egyptian president does not really mean what he says, but that he has to be truculent to calm public opinion. The Israelis, on the other hand, prefer to take Nasser seriously. They say that, even if this charitable explanation should be correct, it would mean that peace is impossible because Nasser and other Arab leaders have to bow to public opinion. And how will public opinion ever change if it is constantly told that only force will bring a solution? But the long-distance rockets are not mere propaganda devices, and there is always the danger that, as he was last year, Nasser (or his successor) may be drawn into a conflict—by the Syrians, by Al Fatah or by his own impetuosity—well before the date that he may envisage now.

Israel may not have missed any diplomatic opportunities since the end of the war, the frame of mind of the Arab governments being what it is. But policies should not exist only with an eye to the present, and the exigencies of national defense should not overrule all other considerations. Israel is a small country and still threatened with extinction; it is not certain how much magnanimity it could have shown after the victory without jeopardizing its existence. On the whole, however, the military operations were better planned than the more distant political campaign. Peace moves should have been made immediately after the war; there was no point in "waiting for Hussein." Though the refugee problem remains a festering sore, no constructive program for its solution has been proposed by the Israeli government during the last year. Negotiations with the Arab governments seem to be impossible now, but it is not at all clear whether a real effort has been made to discover a possible common ground with the Palestinian Arab refugee organizations. These groups—Al Fatah among them—have been the most extreme in their condemnation of Israel, but they have been almost as critical of the Arab governments, including those of Egypt and Syria. Many of their leaders have begun to realize that the most they can hope for is not the destruction of Israel but concessions and a gradual change in its character as a "Zionist state." However unlikely an agreement with the Palestinian Arabs seems at this moment, approaches have to be made with an eye to the more distant future.

The Soviet Union played an unfortunate role, intentionally or unintentionally, in helping to spark last year's war by spreading false rumors. Now, one year later, there is a big Soviet fleet in the Mediterranean and thousands of Soviet military experts are stationed in Egypt. It can be assumed that Moscow asked for, and no doubt received, certain undertakings from Nasser not to use his new weapons without prior consultation. But it is open to doubt whether this would be sufficient to prevent yet another escalation. Nor is it clear whether Moscow is opposed to a new limited war at some future date.

Soviet policy has been defined as selective probing for weak spots in the Western system. To talk about "Soviet policy," is, of course, a simplification; various and sometimes conflicting forces are at work in Moscow. But all Kremlin officials seem to feel, in various degrees of intensity, that something ought to be done to improve the Soviet position in international affairs after the series of setbacks suffered in recent years. Soviet military capability, both conventional and nuclear, has grown during the last years, and the gradual erosion of communism in Eastern Europe provides a strong temptation to undertake action that would restore unity. This could not be done in Europe because a head-on clash with NATO is too much of a risk. The Middle East presents a more ideal probing ground: American commitments in the area are not sufficiently clear, and, in view of the growing resistance to the Vietnam war, it must appear unlikely that America will take on any other major commitment in the foreseeable future. There remains an element of uncertainty about the extent of possible American retreat from the Middle East, but the Russians are less in a hurry than the Arabs. Western intentions will be probed and a decision to move into the area more massively will be taken only if it is reasonably certain that the risks are low; to this extent, at least, the future of the Middle East depends on Washington.

Nor should the psychological moment be underrated: Soviet military leaders seem to be genuinely angry with the

Israelis, for the defeat of the Arabs last year was also, albeit indirectly, a Soviet setback in view of a decade of Soviet military assistance to Egypt and Syria. Israel, it is thought, should be taught a lesson.

Can Russia Stay Out?

Direct Soviet involvement in a fourth round seems at present unlikely, but it cannot be ruled out entirely. What if a fourth round should go wrong? Could Russia again afford to stay out of the battle and see its allies once more defeated? The Russian leaders know that there is no such thing as limited military intervention today. Big-power intervention in the Arab-Israeli conflict, however framed or explained, would immediately transform a local conflict into something infinitely more dangerous. There would be more at stake than the future of Israel and the Arab countries, and everyone would act accordingly. The Soviet government, in a note to Jerusalem one week before the outbreak of the war last year, said it was easy to ignite a fire but it might not be nearly so simple to put the flames out. It is platitude, of course, but nonetheless very true.

A fourth round in the Middle East seems likely; it may come in the not-too-distant future; it will probably be fought with more destructive weapons than last time; it may escalate into a conflict between the super powers. The region has, in other words, the making of a crisis potentially more dangerous than Vietnam. An air of fatality is brooding now over the Middle East; a new initiative is urgently needed, but it will hardly come from Israel or the Arab countries. The Arabs are set to get revenge; Israel will not give up the occupied territories unless the Arabs are ready to make peace. Whether the deadlock could be broken by the United States and the Soviet Union is doubtful, but it is certainly in their power to localize the conflict.

It has long been my belief that the importance of the Middle East in world affairs should not be exaggerated and that peace would be restored only when the big powers began losing interest in the area. This case . . . rests on the assumption that the Middle East is an area of high risks, great costs and dubious returns and that it has been bypassed by strategic, economic and technological developments. The relative unimportance of the Middle East clearly emerged during the second half of last year when the Arab governments tried to bring pressure on the West by stopping oil supplies and keeping the Suez Canal closed. There is a surfeit of oil; after a few weeks the Arab boycott had to be called off. The canal is still closed, but Egypt suffers far more than anyone else from its closure.

A big-power disengagement in the Middle East would help to reduce any conflict there to manageable proportions, but a unilateral Western disengagement would have the opposite effect. The situation resembles the state of affairs in Europe: a case can be made for the gradual dissolution of alliances, but the disintegration of NATO alone, without a parallel weakening of the Eastern alliance, would, to say the least, not be a contribution to peace in Europe. A major conflict can be prevented only if there is agreement between America and the Soviet Union not to intervene. Unless American intentions are made clear, there is a distinct danger that the Russians will misjudge the Western position and go too far in their probing. Suddenly West and East would find themselves locked in a confrontation that neither of them wanted.

The Russians are not unmindful of the risks involved in the Middle Eastern power game: They do not need the oil, and Communist regimes are not likely to spread spontaneously in the area. At best, something like the present Syrian regime—ridden by internal struggles and lacking in mass support—is likely to emerge. In this age of polycentrism, Soviet involvement in the Middle East simply means that the Soviet Union will be burdened by responsibility without real power. A vague and ambiguous policy on the part of the West may have its occasional advantages; at the present stage it is clearly a mistake. There is probably time yet for the

West to explain persuasively and forcefully to Moscow the advantages of nonintervention. But the danger of a major conflict increases with every month of uncertainty: "And behold, the whole herd rushed down the steep bank into the sea, and perished in the waters." The incident, it will be recalled took place at Gadara, a few miles east of the Sea of Galilee. It is now known as the ruins of Um Keis, and it has been the scene of recent fighting.

BIBLIOGRAPHY

An asterisk (*) preceding a reference indicates that the article or a part of it has been reprinted in this book.

Books, Pamphlets, and Documents

Avnery, Uri. Israel without Zionists: a plea for peace in the Middle East. Macmillan. New York. '68.

Badeau, J. S. American approach to the Arab world. Harper. New York. '68.

Ben-Gurion, David. Israel: years of challenge. Holt. New York. '63.

Berger, Morroe. Arab world today. Doubleday. New York. '62.

Bermant, C. I. Israel. Walker. New York. '67.

Churchill, R. S. and Churchill, W. S. The Six Day War. Houghton. Boston. '67.

Dayan, David. Strike first! a battle history of Israel's six-day war; tr. from the Hebrew by Dov Ben-Abba. Pitman. New York. '68.

Dayan, Yael. Israel journal: June, 1967. McGraw. New York. '67.

Diab, M. A. Inter-Arab economic cooperation, 1951-1960. American University. Economic Research Institute. Beirut, Lebanon. '64.

Douglas-Home, Charles. The Arabs and Israel. Bodley Head. London. '68.

Draper, Theodore. Israel and world politics: roots of the third Arab-Israeli war. Viking. New York. '68.

Ellis, H. B. Challenge in the Middle East; Communist influence and American policy. Ronald Press. New York. '60.

Fein, L. J. Politics in Israel. Little. Boston. '67.

Freudenheim, Yehoshu'a. Government in Israel; tr. from the Hebrew by Meir Silverstone and C. I. Goldwater. Oceana. New York. '67.

Friedmann, Georges. The end of the Jewish people? tr. from the French by Eric Mosbacher. Doubleday. New York. '67.

Gervasi, F. H. Case for Israel. Viking. New York. '67.

Glubb, Sir J. B. Empire of the Arabs. Prentice-Hall. Englewood Cliffs, N.J. '65.

Hirschfeld, Burt. A state is born; the story of Israel. Simon & Schuster. New York. '67.

Horowitz, David. Economics of Israel. Pergamon. New York. '67.

Howard, Michael, and Hunter, Robert. Israel and the Arab world: the crisis of 1967. (Adelphi papers no. 41) Institute for Strategic Studies. London. '67.

Huxley, J. S. From an antique land; ancient and modern in the Middle East. Harper. New York. '66.

Kagan, Benjamin. Secret battle for Israel; tr. from the French by Patsy Southgate. World. New York. '66.

Kardouche, G. K. U.A.R. in development; a study in expansionary finance. Praeger. New York. '67.

Kerr, M. H. Arab cold war, 1958-1967; a study of ideology in politics. 2d ed. Oxford University Press. New York. '67.

Khouri, F. J. Arab-Israeli dilemma. Syracuse University Press. Syracuse, N.Y. '68.

Kimche, David, and Bawley, Dan. The sandstorm! the Arab-Israeli war of June 1967: prelude and aftermath. Stein & Day. New York. '68.

Kinross, J. P. D. B. Portrait of Egypt. Morrow. New York. '66.

Kosut, Hal, ed. Israel & the Arabs: the June 1967 war. Facts on File. New York. '68.

Laqueur, W. Z. Road to Jerusalem; the origins of the Arab-Israeli conflict, 1967. Macmillan. New York. '68.

Larkin, Margaret. Hand of Mordechai. Yoseloff. Cranbury, N.J. '68.

Latour, Anny. Resurrection of Israel; tr. from the French by M. S. Summers. World. Cleveland. '68.

Lengyel, Emil. Changing Middle East. Day. New York. '60.

Little, Tom. Modern Egypt. Praeger. New York. '67.

Marshall, S. L. A. Swift sword; the historical record of Israel's victory, June 1967. American Heritage. New York. '67.

O'Brien, P. K. The revolution in Egypt's economic system; from private enterprise to socialism, 1952-1965. Oxford University Press. New York. '66.

Polk, W. R. United States and the Arab world. Harvard University Press. Cambridge, Mass. '65.

Pounds, N. J. G. and Kingsbury, R. C. Atlas of Middle Eastern affairs. Methuen. Toronto. '66.

Prittie, C. F. Israel: miracle in the desert. Praeger. New York. '67.

Rivlin, Benjamin, and Szyliowicz, V. S. eds. Contemporary Middle East: tradition and innovation. Random House. New York. '65.

Rodinson, Maxime. Israel and the Arabs. Pantheon. New York. '68.

Rosenthal, Gabriella, and Kallmann, E. A. Israel. Hill & Wang. New York. '66.

Samuel, Maurice. Light on Israel. Knopf. New York. '68.
Sanders, Ronald. Israel; the view from Masada. Harper. New York. '66.
Sedar, Irving and Greenberg, H. S. Behind the Egyptian sphinx; Nasser's strange bedfellows: prelude to World War III? Chilton. Philadelphia. '60.
Sharabi, H. B. Nationalism and revolution in the Arab world (the Middle East and North Africa). Van Nostrand. Princeton, N.J. '65.
Snyder, Z. K. The Egypt game. Atheneum. New York. '67.
Stavrianos, L. S. Middle East; a culture area in perspective. Allyn. Boston. '66.
Stewart-Robinson, James, ed. Traditional Near East. Prentice-Hall. Englewood Cliffs, N.J. '66.
Thomas, Hugh. Suez. Harper. New York. '67.
Thompson, J. H. and Reischauer, R. D. eds. Modernization of the Arab world. Van Nostrand. Princeton, N.J. '66.
Thornburg, M. W. People and policy in the Middle East; a study of social and political change as a basis for U.S. policy. Norton. New York. '64.
Tunstall, John. Vanishing kingdoms. Nelson. New York. '66.
Wallace, Sir D. M. Egypt and the Egyptian question. Russell & Russell. New York. '67.
Warburg, J. P. Crosscurrents in the Middle East. Atheneum. New York. '68.
Waterfield, Gordon. Egypt. Walker. New York. '67.
Yale, William. Near East; a modern history. rev. ed. University of Michigan Press. Ann Arbor. '68.
Zwibak, Jacques. This land of Israel; by Andrei Sedych [pseud.]; tr. by E. R. Hapgood. Macmillan. New York. '67.

PERIODICALS

America. 116:802. Je 3, '67. Commitment to Israel.
Atlantic. 216:24+. Ag. '65. Atlantic report: dividing the waters.
*Atlantic. 219:38+. Ap. '67. Persian Gulf. Martin Page.
*Atlantic. 220:62-9. N. '67. In the wake of war; time and reality in the Middle East. B. W. Tuchman.
*Atlantic. 220:102-4+. D. '67. The Arabs, 1967. J. S. Badeau.
*Atlantic. 221:10+. Ap. '68. Reports: Egypt.
*Bulletin of the Atomic Scientists. 23:12-19. Ja. '67. Middle East: analyzing social change. W. R. Polk.
Business Week. p 25-6. My. 27, '67. Nasser lights fuse.
Business Week. p 29-30. Je. 3, '67. Mideast fuse still sputters.

Business Week. p 164. Je. 3, '67. Middle East crisis.

Business Week. p 35-6, 192. Je. 10, '67. Back from the brink [with editorial comment].

Business Week. p 112-14. Je. 17, '67. Backlash of defeat roils Arab world.

Business Week. p 182. Je. 24, '67. Foreign policy: a study in contrasts; U.S. and U.S.S.R.

Business Week. p 160. Ja. 27, '68. Liquidation of the empire.

Christian Century. 84:708. My. 31, '67. Thunder over Sinai.

Commentary. 44:19-48. Ag. '67. Israel and world politics. Theodore Draper.

Commentary. 44:49-59. Ag. '67. Israel, the Arabs, and world opinion. Walter Laqueur.

*Commentary. 45:41-7. Mr. '68. Israeli occupation. Amos Elon.

*Commentary. 45:49-53. Mr. '68. New status quo. Shlomo Avineri.

Commonweal. 86:382-3. Je. 23, '67. Middle East in crisis. William Pfaff.

Commonweal. 86:406-7. Je. 30, '67. Futility in the Middle East. W. V. Shannon.

Current History. 48:257-301+. My. '65. Middle East 1965: symposium.

*Current History. 52:65-6+. F. '67. Changing of the guard in the Middle East. H. L. Hoskins.

Current History. 52:67. F. '67. Middle East: a broad view.

Current History. 52:84-9+. F. '67. Political trends in Iraq and Kuwait. Majid Khadduri.

Department of State Bulletin. 56:870-3. Je. 12, '67. United States calls for restraint in the Near East; statements, May 23-24, 1967. L. B. Johnson; A. J. Goldberg.

Department of State Bulletin. 56:920-9. Je. 19, '67. U.N. Security Council continues consideration of the crisis in the Near East; statements, May 29-31, 1967. A. J. Goldberg.

Encounter (London). 29:3-14. N. '67. Moment of truth. Cecil Hourani.

*Encounter (London). 30:16-20. F. '68. Strategy of a war. B. H. Liddell Hart.

*Encounter (London). 30:31-3. F. '68. Bitter victory. David Marquand.

Encounter (London). 30:34-7. F. '68. Kiss-and-make-up delusion. Nora Beloff.

*Encounter (London). 30:37-9. F. '68. Maalesh! Inshallah! M. A. Shaban.

Foreign Affairs. 42:123-36. O. '63. Near Eastern nationalism yesterday and today. Albert Hourani.

Foreign Affairs. 46:304-46. Ja. '68. Arab-Israeli war: how it began. C. W. Yost; Bernard Lewis; Don Peretz.

Fortune. 76:71-2. Jl. '67. Real news on the hot line.

Life. 62:4. Je. 9, '67. Hatreds, tensions and theatrics.

Life. 62:40-1. Je. 9, '67. In the Middle East, blockade and face-off.

Life. 62:80-4+. Je. 16, '67. Birth of a nation, roots of the hatred.

Life. 62:87. Je. 16, '67. Arab unity thwarted by old enmities.

Life. 62:20-24C. Je. 23. '67. Armor churns up the Syrian hills. T. H. White.

Life. 62:24-5. Je. 30, '67. Argument indeed: Soviet attack, Israeli retort: with excerpts from addresses. A. N. Kosygin; Abba Eban.

Life. 64:28-31. F. 2, '68. Mideast: U.S. is playing with fire; excerpt from interview, ed. by Hedley Donovan and others. A. N. Kosygin.

    Excerpt. Time. 91:27. F. 2, '68.

Life. 64:66-8+. Ap. 5, '68. Target of the Israeli thrust: Al Asifa, Storm of terror. George De Carvalho.

Middle East Journal. 22:45-57. Winter '68. Israel's new Arab dilemma. Don Peretz.

Nation. 204:706-7. Je. 5, '67. Third front. Anne Weill-Tuckerman.

Nation. 204:770-1. Je. 19, '67. Great de-mythification. Anne Weill-Tuckerman.

National Review. 19:561. My. 30, '67. Explosive triangle. James Burnham.

National Review. 19:562+. My. 30, '67. Countdown in the Middle East; symposium.

National Review. 19:679. Je. 27, '67. Israel to the rescue of the U.S. W. F. Buckley Jr.

New Republic. 156:1-3. Je. 3, '67. Nasser and Israel.

    Discussion. New Republic. 156:34. Je. 24, '67.

New Republic. 156:8-10. Je. 10, '67. Report from Israel. Alex Campbell.

New Republic. 156:inside cover. Je. 17, '67. T. R. B. from Washington; this is the Middle East.

New Republic. 156:3-4. Je. 24, '67. After the victory.

New Statesman. 75:442-5. Ap. 5, '68. Israel and the occupied lands. Naomi Shepherd.

*New York Times. p E 4. Ap. 21, '68. De Gaulle woos the Arabs. Henry Tanner.

*New York Times. p 16. My. 2, '68. After 2 decades and 3 wars, diverse land of Israel is still trying to find its way. James Feron.

*New York Times. p 2. My. 15, '68. Intense economic and political strains beset Iraq. Drew Middleton.

*New York Times. p 1. Jl. 15, '68. Arab world: guerrilla war a way of life. Drew Middleton.

*New York Times. p 1. Jl. 16, '68. Arab world: Soviet role widens. Drew Middleton.

New York Times Magazine. p 24-5. S. 22, '63. Mideast struggle over Yemen.

New York Times Magazine. p 42+. O. 6, '63. 'Al Baath' challenges Nasser; political party that rules Syria and Iraq. D. A. Schmidt.

*New York Times Magazine. p 23+. O. 27, '63. Iran's shah leads a "white revolution." Jay Walz.

*New York Times Magazine. p 22+. N. 3, '63. Middle East paradox—the "beggar rich." F. M. Esfandiary.

New York Times Magazine. p 30-1+. Ag. 28, '66. Watermelon village races against time. Hedrick Smith.

New York Times Magazine. p 7+. Je. 18, '67. Short war and the long war. E. O. Stillman.

New York Times Magazine. p 7+. Jl. 2, '67. Cairo diary: by a Times correspondent. Eric Pace.

New York Times Magazine. p 24-5+. Ap. 7, '68. Hussein approaches "a point of no return." C. B. Pepper.

*New York Times Magazine. p 34-5+. My. 5, '68. Middle East is potentially more dangerous than Vietnam. Walter Laqueur.

*New York Times Magazine. p 32-4+. Je. 2, '68. Year after the six-day war, Israel still finds that in victory there is no peace. Amnon Rubinstein.

New Yorker. 43:96+. Je. 17, '67. Letter from London; House of Lords debate. Mollie Panter-Downes.

*New Yorker. 43:114+. Je. 17, '67. Letter from Israel. Renata Adler.

*New Yorker. 43:84+. Je. 24, '67. Letter from Paris. Genêt.

*New Yorker. 43:90+. Je. 24, '67. Letter from Washington. Richard Rovere.

Newsweek. 69:52. My. 15, '67. Anyone for cribbage? two U.S. foreign-aid officials arrested in Yemen.

Newsweek. 69:40+. My. 29, '67. Razor's edge.

Newsweek. 69:40+. Je. 5, '67. Middle East: the scent of war.

Newsweek. 69:23. Je. 12, '67. Buried meaning of a crisis. E. J. Hughes.

Newsweek. 69:25-6. Je. 12, '67. Strait that pinches big powers.

Newsweek. 69:34. Je. 12, '67. Continuing cold war. Kenneth Crawford.

Newsweek. 69:38+. Je. 12, '67. Intermission: too late and too early.

Newsweek. 69:31-4. Je. 19, '67. Diplomatic counterpoint.

Newsweek. 69:18-20. Je. 26, '67. Biggest pie-throwing contest ever? emergency session of the U.N. General Assembly.

Newsweek. 71:44-7+. My. 13, '68. Israel at twenty: up from a dream.

Reporter. 36:18. Je. 15, '67. U.S. absence. Max Ascoli.

Reporter. 36:19-23. Je. 15, '67. Story of forty-eight hours; U Thant's part in UNEF withdrawal. Meg Greenfield.

Reporter. 37:22-5. Jl. 13, '67. Economics of triumph; post-war economic, political and security headaches. Alvin Rosenfeld.

*Saturday Evening Post. 240:62-3. Jl. 29, '67. Letter from Cairo. Trevor Armbrister.

Saturday Review. 50:20+. Je. 24, '67. What have we learned? Norman Cousins.

Saturday Review. 50:11. Ag. 12, '67. Struggle for power: US-USSR influences. Henry Brandon.

Senior Scholastic. 91:10. O. 5, '67. Fact sheet on the Middle East.

Time. 87:30. F. 11, '66. Tiger at the helm.

*Time. 87:45. Je. 24, '66. Saudi Arabia: revolution from the throne.

Time. 89:37. My. 5, '67. Misguided monarch: ex-King Saud's visit to Yemen.

Time. 89:36. My. 12, '67. Incurable arsonist: Nasser's fight to win absolute control over the Arab world.

Time. 89:38. My. 19, '67. King's plight; state visit of Saudi Arabia's King Feisal to Britain.

Time. 89:26+. My. 26, '67. Sound & fury; troubles on Israeli frontiers.

Time. 89:11-12. Je. 2, '67. Staving off a second front.

Time. 89:20-2. Je. 2, '67. Week when talk broke out.

Time. 89:29-30. Je. 9, '67. Test of patience & resolve.

Time. 89:38-42. Je. 9, '67. Nation under siege.

Time. 89:15-17. Je. 16, '67. Hot-line diplomacy; use of link between Washington and Moscow.

Time. 89:23-4. Je. 30, '67. Divided in defeat; Arabs receive more Russian arms.

Time. 90:24-5. Jl. 7, '67. Picking up the pieces.

U.S. News & World Report. 62:8. My. 29, '67. Exploding conflict in the Mideast.

U.S. News & World Report. 62:19. Je. 5, '67. Did U Thant bungle the Middle-East crisis?

U.S. News & World Report. 62:19-20. Je. 5, '67. Nasser the trouble-maker: what he is up to now.

U.S. News & World Report. 62:29-31. Je. 5, '67. Where next big war can strike.

U.S. News & World Report. 62:30. Je. 5, '67. Back from the brink?

U.S. News & World Report. 62:32-5. Je. 5, '67. Region slipping to Russia, and U.S. has a big stake. John Law.

U.S. News & World Report. 62:40-1. Je. 5, '67. Israel in time of crisis: a report from the scene. W. MacDougall.

U.S. News & World Report. 62:8. Je. 12, '67. Cooling the Mideast: White House role.

U.S. News & World Report. 62:32-5. Je. 12, '67. If Egypt does fight Israel: who wins?

U.S. News & World Report. 62:35-6. Je. 12, '67. What Nasser has won by his threats. John Law.

U.S. News & World Report. 62:48-9. Je. 19, '67. Mideast war's effect on U.S. business.

U.S. News & World Report. 62:112. Je. 19, '67. It's an ill wind. David Lawrence.

Vital Speeches of the Day. 33:452-5. My. 15, '67. Is peace possible? address. F. B. Morse.

DATE DUE

JAN 27 '71			
FEB 9 '71			
MAR 8 '71			
APR 1 9 '71			
FEB 2 6 '73			
MR 1 2 '79			
MR 2 7 '79			
AP 15 '81			
MAR 1 8 '85			
APR 2 1 '85			
GAYLORD			PRINTED IN U.S.A.